CHIEF

Champion of the Everglades

A biography of
Seminole Chief James Billie

Barbara Oeffner

123846

Dedicated to my husband Thom
Whose light guided me and love led me

This book was published by:
Cape Cod Writers, Inc
Post Office Box 621
Palm Beach, Florida 33480
Tel. (407) 820-1406   FAX (813) 946-0348

Library of Congress Number: 95-067410

ISBN number: 0-9645266-0-3

Cover photo of Seminole Chief James Billie by Robb Tiller

Cover design by: Ken Alford of Arts & Graphs, Clewiston, Florida

MANUFACTURED IN THE UNITED STATES OF AMERICA

ii

TABLE OF CONTENTS

Illustrations

Maps

Photographs

Prelude

The first time I saw an Indian was in the East Hampton, Long Island, school auditorium when I was six years old. Chief Thundercloud, who came to our assembly to put on a show for the elementary school, was dressed in buckskin trousers and beaded moccasins with a red feathered headdress that was magnificent. He carried a drum which he beat loudly, much to our enjoyment. He cried war cries up and down the aisles. He waved his tomahawk wildly. The only thing missing was a horse, but I'm sure the principal forbade that much authenticity. He told us the history of the Indians of his Chippewa tribe.

Chief Thundercloud came to our school several times. Once he brought his son, Standing Bear, who was also dressed in a feathered headdress.

Then once in the summertime, I went to my first Indian powwow at the Shinnecock Indian reservation. There were dances by the Indians. They told stories about themselves. They sold Indian handicrafts. They dressed in brightly colored clothes. Little did I realize at the time that this behavior was strictly showmanship for tourists.

The actual life of an Indian was difficult. Federal regulations dictated how reservations were to be run. Hunting had diminished on eastern Long Island. Life had changed drastically for the Shinnecocks from the days when my ancestors in the 1600's came to East Hampton, New York. The Shinnecocks were friendly Indians. For the most part, they traded with whites and left other Indian tribes alone.

There is a canal in Southhampton named the Shinnecock Canal, and an area of land called Shinnecock Hills. The Shinnecocks are a state recognized Indian tribe, not a federally recognized tribe. They did not sign a treaty with the United States, or form any other type of trust relationship.

My family, the Dominys, settled in a place they called Dominy point. No one is sure where that is now. When they moved from Dominy point, they dug up their dead relatives and moved them to a cemetery now known as the Dominy cemetery on Acabonic road. Several other Dominys, my grandfather John Forest and my grandmother Lena are buried in the town cemetery next to town pond in East Hampton.

My grandfather was in the lifesaving service before it was called the Coast Guard. His father was the captain of the service and worked at the Coast Guard station on Georgica Beach. He and my grandmother ran a boarding house on Lily Pond Lane for many years after he retired.

My genealogy is well-documented, thanks to Jeannette Rattray, the owner of the *East Hampton Star,* who researched all of East Hampton's early families and published a book about it in the 1950's. But what about those Indians? Who kept track of them?

Even in the best of circumstances, information is lost on family history. From the 1600's, Dominys kept records of all the clocks they made and the prices they brought. Their business records are indisputable. But I'd like to know, where is Dominy Point? It's not on any map of East Hampton, Long Island, New York.

Carl Yazstremski came to my high school one day to talk about baseball. I wrote a story for my high school newspaper, the *Bonac Beachcomber.* I became interested in journalism and went on to earn a degree from Northwestern University's Medill School of Journalism.

I worked as a copywriter and film guide editor for Encyclopedia Britannica Educational Corporation in Chicago. Then I moved to Cape Cod where I lived for 20 years. My first husband Mike and I raised Brendan and Amie on a horse farm. We renovated a 150-year-old house on historic Route 6A in Cummaquid, Massachusetts. I was Public Relations Director for R. C. Eldred's auction gallery in E. Dennis.

I edited *Sandscript,* a literary magazine published by Cape Cod Writers, Inc. for eighteen years. In 1987, I travelled around the world partly for pleasure and partly to attend a writer's conference in Brisbane, Australia with two other American writers.

When Robb Tiller suggested writing a book about an Indian Chief, my curiousity was immediately sparked. The information-gathering for this biography has been an incredible adventure. As a member of the Daughters of the American Revolution, Seminole Chapter, I have always been intrigued by genealogy.

There are many people I wish to thank. My husband Thom spent countless hours listening to interviews. Patricia Packard helped with the research. My daughter Amie Dunning was my proofreader.

Chief James Billie provided several sources that were invaluable to me. His girlfriend Leslie Garcia provided information about their personal life. Micco, his son, charmed us all.

My thanks to the Depot Museum in Lake Wales, Florida for their helpful exhibit on the Seminoles. There are many people whose help with this book was invaluable. I am grateful to Betty Mae Jumper, Winifred Tiger, Joel Frank, Osley Saunooke, Neil MacMillan, Nina and Pete Turner, Bert and Rita Crowell, Bob and Rita Dion, Laura Mae Osceola, Paul Simmons, Swamp Owl, Jack Skelding, Roy Diamond, Bob Grant, John Roberts, Dave, Barbara and Kenny Vopnford, Maria Califano, Phil and Sonya Genovar, Dr. Jim Fatigan, Pat Wickman, Neil MacMillan, Carol Stanley, Chuck Billie, Ard and Georgia Turner, John and Berthe Grayson, Blanche Oeffner, Lou Coviello, Susan Dion, Roger Alden, Bryan Cohen, John White, Leif Vopnford, Ellen Roberts, my agent Carolyn Gilbert and all the other people involved.

Skeets and Denise Johns and their children Jennifer "Yo-lee" — Fox and Danny "Kah-hang-gee" — Deer, trusted me with their wedding photo taken under the Kapok tree. James was their best man. Jimmy McDaniels shared his experiences as wildlife biologist for the Florida Fish and Game Commission for 31 years.

This book is the result of countless interviews, much observation, and hours of research. It is a biography that I hope is as fascinating to you as it was to me while I was working on it.

Putting together the pieces of someone's life is like a treasure hunt. There are statements made by one person that fit into the total picture much like a puzzle. Each story about the person is slowly assembled until the photograph comes into focus. When the interviews are over, the story must be told in a readable way. Chief James Billie's biography is a continuing saga of the battles fought by the Seminole Tribe of Florida. It is an inspiring story and has changed my life forever. In every person's search for his roots, facets of what made him outstanding are revealed. The Native American story is a part of America's history that should be cherished. Chief James Billie is a hero to his tribe and an inspiration to everyone. He is a true Champion of the Everglades.

Part I

Chief James Billie:
THE BIOGRAPHY

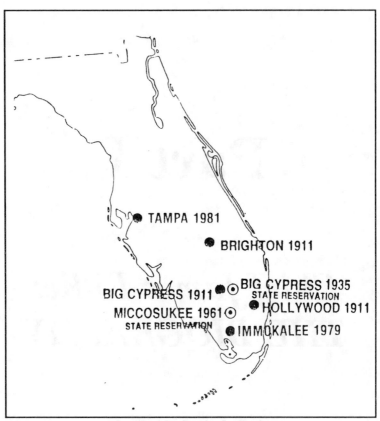

TAMPA 1981

BRIGHTON 1911

BIG CYPRESS 1935
STATE RESERVATION

BIG CYPRESS 1911

HOLLYWOOD 1911

MICCOSUKEE 1961
STATE RESERVATION

IMMOKALEE 1979

The Florida Seminole Nation

x

Chapter 1

The Seminole Swamp

There is an old saying around the Everglades: if you take a seed and step on it, it will grow overnight into a tree that is over your head. The Everglades soil is blacker than coal and more fertile than a rabbit. The sun warms the fresh water gator holes where gopher turtles breed. Bald eagles fish in the Caloosahatchee and Kissimmee Rivers. Large mouth bass troll the rivers and lakes. Alligators flourish here in the steamy heat of woods, pastures and swamps. Gray manatees play in the rim canal of Lake Okeechobee.

Hurricane Andrew blew away many trees here where the Everglades birds nested. Woodpeckers tap loudly on a dead oak in a diligent search for insects. Bred in captivity then released, woodstorks do not know enough to sleep in canals for protection at night, making them easy prey for panthers, bobcats and coyotes.

There is a harmony between the Seminoles and their swamp. They build their chickees on firm cabbage palm hammocks amid the cattails and sawgrass. Indian canoes ply along the rivers, transporting them in that slow, dependable form of travel they have relied on for centuries.

1

It is no wonder then that the Seminoles are the only Indian tribe never to have signed a peace treaty. Their mosquito-riddled swamp is not for weaklings. Brains and muscle are the tools necessary for enduring this watery prairie full of alligators, snakes, biting insects and wild boar.

Lacking natural predators other than man, the Florida crocodile keeps to itself in three breeding grounds: Everglades National Park, north Key Largo and beside a nuclear power plant. This reptile is a cousin to the once endangered alligator which has now come back from the over-hunting that nearly annihilated the species.

The bear, wolves and panthers that once lived in the swamps are also nearly gone. The snail kite is endangered. The herds of deer that used to bound through the cypress trees and cabbage palms are greatly reduced. Wild turkeys are now a rarity. Changes have crept over the Everglades, shrinking the native species with each encroaching sugar cane field and citrus grove.

The flooding that occurs annually on the Big Cypress reservation in the heart of the Everglades still washes the porous soil. The Indian land hasn't changed as much as some of the other parts of the glades, isolated as it is from the housing developments creeping out from Ft. Lauderdale and the cane fields owned by the U.S. Sugar Company. The abundant supply of wildlife that supported the Native Americans and kept the Seminoles free is dwindling.

Two bald eagles nest year after year in the top branches of an Australian pine near the levee surrounding Lake Okeechobee. The lake provides fish for the young eaglets and osprey that festoon the branches.

Named Gertrude and Heathcliff by the South Bay residents, the eagles return every winter to their aerie overlooking the best bass lake in the country to raise their young eaglets in a nest made of sticks and vines. A strong wind occasionally blows their nest out of the tree but the plentiful food trade-off seems to be worth the risk to them.

Morning doves act out a mating dance on the rooftop of a house in Moore Haven, on the west edge of the Big 0. Their display attracts the fleeting attention of a neighborhood dog, but they continue fluttering their wings in a wondrous ritual. Afternoon brings a thunderstorm with lightning that illuminates the dark thunderheads over the Lake.

The Seminoles get their sense of time from the rhythm of the Everglades. There is no down time here, no winter respite from the virulent growth. Palm trees, maples, cypress trees, Australian pines and melaleuca mark the perimeters of the fields and pastures. Growing up in the glades, Seminole Indians feel a closeness to nature in line with the constantly throbbing environment. The sun rises and sets, transforming the blue sky into a golden kaleidoscope of purple, orange and magenta. The farms grow an abundance of corn like they have for ages. The Everglades has been a haven from enemies, a source of food and a wellspring of resilience to the Seminoles.

The construction of 1,400 miles of canals and levees has altered the breeding environment of wading birds to their serious detriment. Their annual nesting season once began at the beginning of the dry season in November. Now, however, they wait until late February or March. Unfortunately, since the wet season begins in early summer, the ready supply of trapped fish in the ponds disappears when the fledglings are hungriest. This late start means starvation for the young birds.

Deck shoes are the wrong equipment to wear at Big Cypress reservation. Boots are necessary to keep the pygmy rattlers at bay. Long pants help keep off the insects. Light cotton clothing is coolest in the summer heat. A Seminole woman has an open wound the size of a peach. She never felt the snake bite on her ankle, which caused her entire foot to swell.

When the moon rises, a whole new stage is set in the Everglades. Now a curtain rises on the nocturnal animation. Red-shouldered hawks flit over the cypress trees which form high hammocks in the glades. Huge brown owls emerge from the swamps like hooting will-o-the-wisps and perch on treetops or buildings like ghostly phantoms from the dark side of what Mayan Indians believed was the dangerous underworld. Magnificent frigate birds soar over schools of fish in the Atlantic down in the keys. Omniscient mosquitoes appear from the swampy canals.

Precursors of darkness, the no-see-ums come out; black stinging dots. Palmetto bugs, or cockroaches that fly, crawl out of the palm hammocks and cattails. An army of fire ants, stingers at the ready, bites its way through the dense undergrowth of vines crawling with juicy insects. Giant cicadas devour the verdant growth of leafy oaks.

Rat snakes hunt their prey, while indigos, sleepy during the daytime tropical sun, come alive at night. They slither through the sawgrass, alert and ready to dig their fangs into a passing rodent. Cottonmouth snakes float on the black waters, ready to gobble up the slithery minnows.

Danger is there in all its many guises. The harvest

moon backlights a raccoon raid on a garbage can. A mother, her black eyes darting protectively, leads her babies in their furtive forage for dinner, scavengers ready to help themselves to leftovers. Armadillos dig holes in the mucky soil. Spiders weave their sticky webs to trap glades grasshoppers. All night long the caravan plays out a wondrous symphony of sounds. The harsh law of the Everglades is to find your niche in the ecology of the swamplands or be done in by them. A natural order emerges: kill or be killed.

Sometimes the violence is difficult to fathom. In the Everglades, the stark reality paints a picture of the Seminoles' strong will to survive. Like sisal fiber, formed tough because it has to break through rocky soil to grow, the Seminole character has been molded by the struggle to conquer this hostile homeland.

Yet the Everglades can also be gentle. Butterflies gravitate towards hibiscus blossoms. Bumble bees the size of cherry tomatoes flit after honey to store in their honeycombs. Abundant sweet grasses fill the acres and acres of pastureland. Lovely wildflowers saturate the woods with their delicate perfumes.

Citrus is popping up where there used to be swampland. Dole, Coca-Cola Foods and Duda are some of the companies along with the granddaddy of them all, United States Sugar. (Recently students piled bags of sugar around the Florida State Corporate Seal in Tallahassee to protest the stalled Everglades Cleanup Bill which finally won approval.)

Cattle are everywhere—content to graze on the tender grasses of pasture land springing up in the lush green fields. They must be given shots every year against

5

disease. A liquid insecticide dip is poured over their backs to protect them from bites.

Young calves are especially vulnerable. They are helpless when first born. The flocks of vultures will peck out their eyes if there is no one to chase them off. The mother cows are not much help. Cattlemen must supervise their herds incessantly or risk the loss of a significant number of newborns.

Toughened cowboys ride the circuit, working at the different pastures throughout the glades to help with the annual roundup. Cattle horns are clipped with a device similar to a hedge clipper. Genitals are cut off the males and their ear tips are sliced off with a very sharp knife. The new calves are then branded. Continual mooing accompanies this whole procedure.

The cow squeeze is an electrically powered device that secures the animal so that he can be processed. The calves are first sorted out from the rest of the herd. This is because the calf is so small. Occasionally his hooves are caught along with his head. Sometimes a calf nearby makes it through and the shoot captures him around the waist instead of at the neck.

After a year the steers are sold to local buyers. Winn Dixie supermarket bought an animal from a Moore Haven boy, prompting a thank-you ad in the *Clewiston News*.

The tradition of cattle-raising in the Everglades goes back to the 1930's when the Bureau of Indian Affairs agent decided it would be a good source of revenue for the Seminoles. First Brighton reservation supported a successful herd. Cattle ranching as a profitable enterprise grew and spread to Big Cypress.

Seminole cowboys process the calves every year.
Chief Billie (center) holds on.

Hogs were owned by every family at Brighton. The animals were a good source of income because they lived off the wild nuts and cabbage palm berries available on reservation land. They were inoculated against cholera by the Glades County agricultural agent.

While the men were busy with ranching, Seminole women worked as vegetable pickers on farms or picked huckleberries to sell in West Palm Beach and other towns. The berries were sold for five cents a quart, remembers Jack Thomas, a West Palm Beach resident since the 1920's.

7

The gumbo limbo tree, a terra cotta barked tree native to this area, shades the land crabs that scuttle beneath its branches. Sleek otters burrow under the earth to cool off and feast on worms and juicy grubs. Florida holly blooms along the highways, and spreads wildly in the moist drainage canals. Occasionally, an unlucky car or truck skids off the wet pavement into those canals where, too often, the people drown.

Royal poinciana or "tourist trees" open orange umbrellas across the landscape. Water hyacinths clog the lakes and rivers, thrusting their lilac and yellow blossoms up into the mosquito-ridden air. Islands of them break loose in the Lake Okeechobee current and float freely downstream until they are pinioned by a fallen rock or tree.

In the last decade, the pulse of the Everglades has quickened. Skunks spray their distinctive odor into the panoply of swamp smells. Jacaranda, a tree with beautiful purple flowers, adds a shock of color to the greenness of the landscape. Pink and white oleanders sprout up into trees.

Much to the delight of environmentalists who have gone to great lengths to protect them, pairs of mating eagles are gradually increasing in number. For example, building was halted on a Marco Island subdivision while a pair of eagles raised two healthy babies. Eagles are now mating in urban areas such as landfills, city parks, in residential neighborhoods and even near busy highways. One pair hatched two thriving chicks just off a Winter Park country club golf course.

Pods of dolphins frolic in the warm waters of the Atlantic north of Everglades National Park. Brookfield zoo sponsors a breeding facility on Duck Key to maintain the dolphin population and do scientific research on the species.

Cowboys snooze under their horse trailers, out of the blazing noonday sun. Toughened to the physical labor, they grab a midday siesta, knowing the afternoon routine will continue with grueling work. Everyone is waiting for the veterinarian, who was supposed to show up at noon.

The oldest person there is Leslie Garcia's grandmother. She remembers roundups from long ago when her husband owned a cattle herd. She is dressed in the traditional Seminole patchwork skirt and colorful shoulder-length cape. She sits contentedly lost in her memories on the tailgate chuck wagon, happy to watch the familiar events of the roundup unfold before her eyes.

"She's very independent. She lives by herself," explains Leslie's mother. "She always lets you know if she wants to do something. You don't have to ask her twice." A proud woman, the Seminole grandmother still sells hamburgers from her cart to passing tourists during the week.

The Everglades, like the Seminole character, is adaptable to the intrusions of the outside world. It retains its uniqueness, while constantly evolving, constantly changing. This ability to change slowly has maintained a special place in history for the Seminoles because they fought and died to stay in the swamps that they love. The Everglades are an integral part of their folklore, their traditions, and their very soul.

Leslie Garcia's grandmother

Chapter 2

A Son of the Glades

On the 1700's, the Seminoles lived in relative harmony with other Indian tribes. The 1800's brought radical changes to their hunting and farming way of life. Intrusion from whites and blacks—the first looking for settlement land and the latter seeking to escape slavery—altered the complexion of Florida.

To think of the Seminoles as one tribe is a relatively recent phenomenon. Actually they were composed of several family groups scattered throughout the state. Those groups were known by such names as Bowlegs Town and Fowltown. These Indians were very mobile. They lived in small settlements, usually on a river or near a lake. As an example, the Fowltown Indians moved to Lake Miccosukee to escape from white soldiers.

Life was easy for the average Indian in Florida until Andrew Jackson came along. Wanting to make a name for himself as an Indian fighter in 1818, he marched his troops 450 miles from Tennessee to Fort Scott near Pensacola in 46 days. The soldiers were mostly undeterred in Florida because they outnumbered the Seminoles by roughly ten to one. His force consisted of about 3,500 white men, mostly soldiers, facing 350 Seminoles.

After marching his men to Ft. Marks, Jackson battled both the Seminoles and the blacks. Jackson and his men then moved toward Pensacola, concluding the First Seminole War.

The plan to concentrate the Seminoles in the Florida interior was hatched in 1823. The Secretary of War, John C. Calhoun, commissioned James Gadsden to carry this out.

The Seminoles were to receive $6,000 in livestock and farm equipment. The government would also pay the Seminoles $5,000 a year for 20 years.

Gadsden managed to get 32 chiefs to sign the Treaty of Moultrie Creek by allotting certain parcels to Emathlochee, Tuski Hadjo, Neamathla, Mulatto King, Blont, and Econchatimico.

However, the treaty was imposed unfairly. In May, 1964, the Petitioner' Motion for Summary Judgment in the modern Seminole claim decided "Petitioners contest that six chiefs were bribed to sign the Treaty of Moultrie Creek. Therefore, the United States obtained said lands by duress, bribery, unconscionable consideration and by dealings that were not fair and honorable."

In order to seize tribal lands and prevent bloodshed, the U.S. Indian policy under President Andrew Jackson then was to force Indians to move west of the Mississippi River. The Removal Bill was signed on May 28, 1830. Of all the tribes living east of the Mississippi at that time, the fierce Seminoles put up the greatest resistance to removal. The Second Seminole War was expensive. It cost the United States government an estimated $30 to $40 million and the lives of over 1,500 men. The war raged for seven years, and ended only when an estimated 4,000 or more blacks and Seminoles were relocated in Oklahoma. Four to five hundred Seminoles remained behind, refusing to leave their beloved Florida. They hid in the Everglades swamp that shielded them from the grasp of the army's rapacious tentacles.

Born in 1804, Osceola was active and enterprising—the characteristics of a born leader. His father was William Powell, the white trader. His mother was a Muskogee Indian named Polly Copinger.

He arrived at Tampa Bay as a scout when he was about 21 to lead a party of horsemen. He strolled along for a while—Florida Indians then rarely used horses. The men followed slowly. Osceola asked the interpreter why they were riding at a walk. The answer came that it was because Osceola wasn't riding.

"Tell them not to be slow for me," Osceola said, smiling. "I can stay with them."

Grinning when this was translated, the horsemen urged their mounts to trot and sometimes, on open fields, to gallop. Osceola amazed them by keeping up with them on foot and laughing at their astonishment. When the riders slowed their horses down, they noticed that Osceola was not even out of breath. Osceola regarded his challenge as an excellent joke.

This chase kept up all day. At dusk Osceola was such a great athlete that he showed no symptoms of fatigue even though he arrived at the point proposed at the same time as the horsemen.

Known as the unconquered Indian, Osceola set a standard of loyalty and integrity for the Seminoles. He earned his reputation as a war chief through many years of fighting. He spoke eloquently and passionately with the skill of a seasoned politician.

The Treaty of Moultrie Creek had assured the Seminoles their land for twenty years. Chiefs Jumper, Micanopy and Charley Emathla rallied together to say that they had not intentionally signed an agreement to go to the west, but had only said that the land was good.

"The government would send us among tribes with which we could never be at rest," Chief Jumper said.

Agent Thompson called them fools and said he needed to know whether they would travel by land or water. The Secretary of War endorsed a peaceful removal, which gave the Seminoles additional time to accumulate powder and lead.

Osceola's response was brutal. He killed Charley Emathla, a Seminole who led a band of 450 people ready to leave. Charlie's body and the money he had received for his cattle lay for two years on the ground where it fell. Then, during the Dade Massacre, which occurred when a band of Seminoles ambushed 108 soldiers marching towards Fort King, Osceola killed and scalped Agent Thompson and Lieutenant Constantine Smith.

Like the eagles that came back from near extinction, the Seminoles have fought to maintain their birthright to the Everglades. James Billie is the Chief of the Seminoles. Monkeys still roam free in the woods in Dania where baby James came into this world. He can talk to those monkeys because James communicates with animals and people alike. His wisdom allows a quick evaluation of people and animals without wasting gestures or words. His stare is all-knowing as he probes for weaknesses as well as strengths.

This story of the Florida Seminoles is intertwined with the events in James's life. At one time the tribe was deeded all the land in the state of Florida south of Lake

Okeechobee by President James K. Polk. Where the Florida turnpike runs through the Hollywood reservation, James insisted the state landmark the point with a sign saying "Seminole Indian Reservation."

One Seminole prophesy foretold that a white man would come and lead the tribe out of misery to prosperity. Some tribal members say that James is that man. A half-breed, he was ostracized as a child. He fought hard to be accepted in both the Indian and the white worlds. This tenacity is an inherited trait of the Seminole that has served the tribe well. Since James Billie took over as chairman in 1979, the tribe's fortunes have skyrocketed. With his fierce single-mindedness and laser-sharp intelligence, the chief of the Seminoles is wise to the mysteries of the Everglades in ways that come from a deep knowledge of its secrets.

"I think I grew up fast," said Chief Billie. He and his dog, Yellow Eye, roamed the Cabbage Palm ranch and pine forests of Delray Beach before they were built up.

"At home, I was the white boy. At school and in local stores, I was the Indian. I learned to fight."

James Billie was raised by his grandmother and grandfather Tommie Billie and Johnny Buster, as his mother died when he was nine.

The outdoors is where James feels at home. He retreats to the woods to restore his feeling of well-being. It is where he was born and where he will be buried, in a small cemetery not far from the home he built for himself, Leslie, and his son Micco on Big Cypress reservation. The architecture of the house makes it blend naturally into the woods. A 14-foot alligator hide is hung on the wall of the porch and a hammock swings from the wooden posts.

"It gives me a good feeling to know that my placenta was dropped in the ground in the place where I was born near the cut off canal between Hollywood and Dania." Chief Billie would like the tribe to act more like they did in the old days when people would share with each other in communal ways.

He thinks the fascination white people have with the Indian arises from a curiosity about the mystery of fire.

"If you learned how to start a fire by rubbing two sticks together from an Indian, you want to know more," concludes the Indian chief. "People in Europe have been removed from this primitive way of starting a fire for many years."

"My grandfather was telling me that change is bad. I was relieving myself. I said to my grandfather, do you want me to stop what I'm doing right now? My grandfather didn't appreciate my answer."

As a boy, James Billie would go up to the dairy by the pine trees for his milk. With a slingshot around his neck, he and Yellow Eye would hunt in the woods at the time when the last of the steam engines went out.

"The Seminoles have had perseverance," admits Joel Frank, head of the Seminole Gaming Commission. Joel works in Washington, D.C. to administer the bingo-related activities of the tribe.

Unable to resist temptation, James stole his first bicycle. Knowing his grandmother would disapprove, he reported the story with a twist.

"I finally found my father and he gave me a bicycle," said Billie with a straight face. His grandmother wasn't buying that story, but this inventiveness would stand him in good stead.

He and Yellow Eye hunted constantly. "What we brought home was usually what we ate," explained James. This love for hunting and the outdoors has stayed with the chief to this day.

Changes came to Delray Beach in the 1950's. They chopped down the pine trees and laid out a flat piece of smooth grass. James and Yellow Eye lay down on the grass and felt the wind blow past them. Over the wide expanse, it looked like eggs were falling to the ground. Suddenly, an "egg" hit James on the head and left a dent that is still there. The golf course had been added, much to young James' surprise. He didn't know about the game of golf until a ball hit him squarely in the head. Of course, with the country club came a new source of information. The dumpster behind it was full of foods such as chicken, apple pie and even partially empty bottles of liquor.

"I never told Grandma about the food thing," admits James, probably rightly concluding she would put a stop to his picking through the dumpster.

Another observation the area provided was a nearby lovers lane. One of the black people in the neighborhood used the back road for seduction. James found items that looked like balloons that had been discarded in the bushes.

He got his first look at "spanish moss" on a woman when he saw two people humping and rolling around on the ground. It didn't take much imagination to figure out right then what the two were doing. There was a lot of moaning going on.

"Even my dog got an erection," related James. James spied on this lovers lane several times. The men made love to different women on succeeding nights. There was

17

one similarity. "The man always had big huge fat women with him. I wonder why," James mused.

"When I started elementary school, I got my first pair of shoes. They were bought by Neil MacMillan," remembered James.

Although Chief Billie doesn't try to moralize to members of his tribe, he himself is the product of a strict Baptist upbringing. That in later years he questioned this preaching is understandable. In his own words, he has always tested, tested, tested. He is still doing it

The chief deals harshly with belief structures that he finds wanting.

"Don't go to the Green Corn Dance because that's paganism," James was told by the Baptist preacher. The religious dance encompasses the belief that the great spirit comes down and blesses the participants.

His childhood woods have taught him valuable lessons. They have nourished and protected him the way they rescued his Seminole forefathers from oblivion. Early on he learned their secrets. Part of it was instinct. Part of it was observation.

His Seminole heritage helped mold him into the warrior he is today. The most important factor was something intangible—he was and always will be an Indian.

James follows the political tradition blazed by Osceola who refused to be removed from the Everglades by the onerous white men's greed for Seminole land.

One of the Osceola boys was a football hero. He played for Okeechobee. In high school James admired him because he was an Indian. Then he took away James girlfriend.

"You know the Garth Brooks song about that? Another man takes away your girl and then years later, you're glad because she's gained 40 pounds! Am I glad now." Chief Billie likes to laugh. He admires Mark Twain, calling him "a good Seminole boy."

Neil MacMillan recalls the days when he owned the Cabbage Palm Ranch on Germantown Road. Neil is an attorney who was born in Canada and practiced law in Delray Beach. He now has Parkinson's disease and retired in January, 1992 from the practice of law. His daughter, Carol Stanley, carries on his practice.

Johnny Buster and Tommie Billie, James' grandfather and grandmother, lived in a chickee with their grandson. Johnny Buster was a cattleman who did the mowing on Neil's ranch.

John Banting, president of the Chamber of Commerce, owned a store up on Federal Highway in Delray Beach. He told Neil MacMillan that he had an Indian that he knew. Tommy Billie sewed skirts to sell in John Banting's store.

"I think they lived in Delray because he was ostracized. The tribe wouldn't accept him because he was half white," said MacMillan. "I hired Johnny to manage my ranch."

"He was always very self-confident," says Carol Stanley. "Even as a child, he was larger than life."

She met Jimmy Billie when "he could talk, so he must have been four or five. He was very bossy and very athletic. He used to catch wild animals and try to scare me."

"In those days, Delray was a small town. Germantown road was where all the roughnecks lived, but no one worried too much. My parents let us hang out around there. It wasn't like it is today. They knew we'd be O.K. He was a year older than I am, but we acted as if we were the same age. Jimmy was my protector and he looked out for me."

"He could ride anything. He'd just get right on horses that were hard to ride. My friends and I took equestrian lessons to learn to do the diagonals properly but he just figured out how to do them by himself."

"He was never shy. His grandparents and brother Charlie would run and hide. He'd try and help out if we had company. When we had parties, he'd come right over and tell stories. He was just born that way."

"He used to catch possums, gopher turtles, and raccoons. They always had a stew pot going. He could catch snakes and used to chase me with them."

"He would spend time in the canal. There was a huge oak tree out there on the ranch. He would climb up in it."

"I don't know why he didn't like school. He only came about a dozen times all year. He was very well spoken as a child and his grammar was good. He was like a sponge."

The truant officer used to call Neil, but Neil he said he wasn't responsible for Jimmy. Carol was in Jimmy's class. James attended about one day in the whole school year.

"I used to have parties at the ranch. Johnny Buster would help me set up the charcoal fires. Jimmy Billie was popping snakes," remembered Neil MacMillan.

"'Mac, look here,' he called to me proudly.

"'A wildcat scratched me,' he'd yell. Or, on another occasion, 'A rattlesnake bit me.'

"Jimmy was like my boy," said Neil tenderly. "He used to ride the pony and he'd round up the cows.

"'Get out of there, a snake's going to bite you!' he'd warn. 'What's the matter Mac? Are you afraid of snakes?' He'd taunt. He'd make me feel about two inches tall.

"He wasn't scared of anything, according to him," said MacMillan.

"Jimmy was always smart. He said to me, 'I'm going to be chief someday'.

"'What's the first thing you're going to do as chief?' I asked. 'I'm going to kill all the white people,' bragged James.

Johnny Buster operated a model T Ford. One time they picked him up. He was driving slowly but didn't have a license. In court, Attorney MacMillan represented him.

"I told the Judge he can't speak English or read English. He's Seminole. He fined him $100 and I paid it."

"His grandmother was also very kind to us. She did a lot of sewing on a foot peddle sewing machine. She was very shy. They used to eat the cabbage palms that grew on the ranch. The ranch was 400 acres."

"His grandfather used to drive me around on the tractor and help me catch my horse. They were a very close knit family.

"Jimmy liked to ride with no bridle or saddle, just bareback. He was such an athlete!" Carol remembered. "We used to play cowboys and Indians. He played the Indian."

21

"Jimmy always said he was going to be chief. He was proud of his Indian heritage. We went down to Big Cypress with him a few times. But in those days, he said he was going to live with the white man. He liked to drive the tractor on the farm."

Carol Stanley has a photo she took of the Seminole family with her Brownie camera, when Charlie was still in diapers.

"There were a lot of country folk on Germantown Road in those days. They would do a little hunting and fishing. Their parents did odd jobs."

"They used to fight and that sort of thing. Jimmy hung around with them. Lots of them didn't have shoes to wear. They were what we'd call gangs today, but then they didn't get into trouble the way they do today."

"Delray has changed since then. In those days, Delray only had one first grade and one second grade. I guess those roughnecks moved out to Okeechobee," Carol said, commenting on her rural childhood.

When James was eleven, Johnny Buster and Jimmy Billie moved back to the Indian reservation in Hollywood. Not long afterwards, James got restless. Where Route 80 and Route 27 met west of Clewiston, there was a 90 degree turn, which the highway department has since made into a curve. Behind this curve, there were 16 sections of land belonging to Earl Henry.

Nina Turner ran a restaurant and her husband Pete ran the service station on this corner. The Osceola family had a stand nearby where they sold Seminole crafts. At 11, James told his grandfather he was going to stay with the Osceola family at the stand, but he really rode the school bus back and forth with the Osceola children, and slept in one of the junk cars behind the gas station.

"James always had the ability to do what he wanted to do. If he wanted to do something, there was no doubt about it—it would get done! When he started building that restaurant out at the safari there was nothing there. One year later the restaurant was looking like it had been there forever."

"James soon moved to the barn at the Henrys' ranch and stayed in the hayloft. Earl Henry had cowboys staying in the barn too. The cowboys would drink beer and act rowdy.

"Them people are giving me a bad time. They puke all over me and my clothes," James told Pete.

"We had two sets of bunks. So I said to him, 'James, take your stuff over to my house and wash your clothes. You're coming to live here.'"

Nina checked his hair and found lice, which she washed out. "We had 3 boys and a girl at that time. Vian was born in 1945 and Doyle in 1947. We also had a German shepherd," Nina said.

Pete said, "James and Doyle did a lot of hunting together in 1958 and 1959. One day they were going through the swamp with water up to their knees. Doyle told James 'I think I ran into bamboo.' James examined his leg and found the fang marks of a snake. James said to him, 'Be calm and don't get excited. You just do what I tell you to do.' James put Doyle on his shoulder and carried him to firm pasture ground and told him not to move. Then James ran to the gas station and said, 'Tell Harley Dad has to go to the hospital.' James drove the car to the pasture and brought Doyle back to the station, while I called ahead and told the hospital we were coming. We headed to the hospital. When we got to the hospital, we found that a cottonmouth had bitten him. There was a doctor waiting with anti-venom shots and they admitted him to the hospital. Dr. Chute, who performed the exam, said that the only thing that saved Doyle's leg was the way it was handled. If Doyle had tried to walk or run on it, the venom would have spread.

"The next evening James said to me, 'All right Dad, I'm ready for my beating."

"Why should you get a beating?" Pete asked him.

"For taking Doyle out and getting him snake-bit," replied the young James.

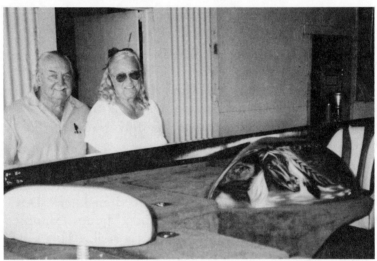

Pete and Nina Turner
admire James' bass boat.

24

Chapter 3

Roots

*I*ronically, the interior swamp land that is now five Seminole reservations has become some of the most valuable land in Florida. Hollywood reservation is located in the heart of Broward County, Immokalee boasts a new Seminole Gaming Palace, accessible from the West Coast, while Tampa provides gaming to a large market in the Tampa bay region. Big Cypress has plans to become a wilderness resort. Brighton contains pasture land and a turtle farm as well as a bingo hall.

The Third and last Seminole War started in 1855 and lasted three years. The objective was to rid Florida of Seminoles. Since there were pockets of the Everglades and Ten Thousand Islands that were completely inaccessible, this goal was never met. However, many Seminoles were relocated.

The leaders of the Seminoles decreed death to those Indians who dealt in any way with the whites. Their clothes tattered, their ammunition so difficult to obtain that they had to dig bullets out of trees the whites used for target practice, the proud Seminoles eluded capture. Part of the reason was the fact that many of the troops were penniless emigrants who had landed in the country on one of the waves of Irish and German immigration.

They had little knowledge of woodcraft and less of life in the swamps. In short, they were no match for the foxy Seminoles. Many were content to lounge and drink their time away.

On May 4, 1858, Billy Bowlegs with 38 men and 85 women and children sailed to Egmont Key from Ft. Myers. Of these, 41 sailed to New Orleans aboard the *Grey Cloud.* On May 8, the end of the Third Seminole War was proclaimed.

On the Hollywood reservation, there was a belief that the Seminoles should keep their race pure. When James Billie was born, the son of a beautiful Seminole girl, Agnes Billie and an Irish American who was a pilot at the local naval base, James' grandfather wanted him put to death.

Half-breeds, to the Indians, were thought to be the doings of evil spirits. They were either drowned or mud was stuffed in their mouths so they suffocated. During the Seminole Wars, there was a period when the children from age 4 to 14 were nonexistent because they would betray their parents' whereabouts.

The Irish, like the Seminoles, are great storytellers. Their attraction for Indians is mysterious yet unmistakable. Chief Billie's father appeared to take out his mother, an Indian maiden. He wooed her with fruit pies from the nearby naval base. In 1944 the country was at war. Agnes and her sister Annie liked to go to the movies. They hitched rides in the liberty truck from passing soldiers going to the matinees.

The two sisters were undoubtedly intrigued at the prospect of dating their first white men. They were not strangers to them, as they were accustomed to seeing tourists at the Seminole attractions that employed the Indians along the main road to Miami.

She flirted with him and he called again. They dated all summer and when she went back to school, Agnes discovered she was pregnant. She was brought home from the Cherokee school by Betty Mae Jumper. Her mother delivered him. Just as Seminole women in the past had tied up their men when they had drunk too much "low bush lightening" (whiskey), Betty Mae rescued baby James. If his grandfather had had his way, young baby James would have been put to death because he was a half-breed. The Seminoles back in the 1940's had a great deal of distrust for white men.

Betty Mae announced to all the members of the Seminole tribe that James Billie had been born. She would later grow up to be Chief herself. Betty Mae knew a certain white officer named J.W. Barnett, who was a naval pilot at the nearby naval base. He showed interest in Agnes Billie.

When he was a small boy, James asked his grandmother where his father was. He knew he had a mother, but had never seen his father. His grandmother told him that his father was a pilot who went to war and got killed in the Philippines.

In later years, when he had the resources, James decided to investigate his bloodline. He asked Pat Wickman, a historian, to find out whether J.W. Barnett was really his father.

"Barnett was surprised when he heard about me. He asked, 'Is he a Christian?'", said the Chief.

When the blood test from J.W. Barnett came back, it was negative. Barnett was not James' father.

On March 20, 1944, James Billie was born. His

mother was not married to his father, a naval pilot who had brought pies to the pretty Seminole maiden. Rumor has it that Billie was conceived under a jeep.

Chief Billie's grandmother was the product of incest. Her father created his grandmother. She was given away in a bundle to a Seminole man who was passing through the swamp. She was strapped on his back so that he could carry her away. The Seminoles called his grandmother a "misfit." As punishment for his crime, which was forbidden, his great grandfather was ordered killed. He was shot twice by another tribal member who knew him well. The man who had been ordered to kill him protested, "But he's my friend!" However, he carried out the execution. He called the man over with a friendly wave. He shot him twice with a gun. After he died, to show disgrace, his body was ordered tied behind a horse and dragged away. The Seminoles felt he had acted like "a dog" and didn't deserve a decent burial. His body was left to be eaten by the buzzards.

Frank Billie, Chief Billie's uncle, was instrumental in organizing the Seminole tribe. He was forward-thinking in his approach, realizing that the white man was here to stay and had to be recognized. He became the first president of the Seminole Tribe of Florida, Inc.

The first chairman of the council was Bill Osceola. Many of the Seminoles back in 1957 were not in favor of organizing. However, the faction geared towards this progress gained the majority.

"I'll never know my father. He got me through a lot. He is this imaginary figurehead who is larger than life. I wanted to go to war because he did," said James.

During World War II, the Seminoles played various roles. They bought $40,000 worth of war bonds. When

Betty Mae Tiger was 19 she purchased the first war bond as a schoolgirl. She attended school at Cherokee, North Carolina with three other Seminoles.

Chief Billie and Ernest Hillard. Micco Billie in foreground.

Chief Billie is a member of the Bird Clan. Their function in the tribe is as keeper of the earth.

"The clan is very important to tribal members," said Chief Billie. "It doesn't mean anything to non-Indians, but it is very significant to us."

Leslie Garcia and James Billie have been together for five years. She is from a family with 6 children, including a twin brother Wesley. Her birthday is June 19, 1972. They have a son, Micco, born on October 5, 1991.

Leslie and James love to go deep sea fishing and diving together on vacations. Leslie recently received her certification in scuba diving.

Leslie's mother is a full-blooded Seminole from the Panther Clan. Her father is Mexican. She was a drum majorette when she and James first met.

Chief Billie still—despite his many obligations—finds time to be in the woods he knows so well. Every year in the fall, James goes hunting in the Northwest woods, and he stays in a cabin in the woods. He loves to ride his Harley motorcycle in the cool weather.

Leslie and Micco

The Everglades affected every aspect of Chief Billie's ancestors' lives. Most of Florida's southeastern tribes planted simple crops of corn or maize, beans, and squash. Hunting and fishing were jobs for the men. Deer was the most important game before the Europeans arrived. The

Indians tanned the hide into leather for clothing and the meat served as nutritious food.

Aboriginal Florida Indians such as the Calusa, the Tequestas, the Jeaga and the Ais were nearly extinct. They had fallen victim to war and disease brought on by the Spanish, French and British colonizers. In the early 1700's, an emigration southward by several thousand Indians of the Creek confederacy to establish settlements caused the repopulation of Florida.

Chief James Billie is grateful for these roots. His proud heritage stems from a firm belief in self-reliance. He is able to create his own story from the bits and pieces he knows about the history of his ancestors.

For two centuries, the battles between white men and the Indians were bitter. Blood was shed relentlessly. In the tradition of Osceola, James' courage and independence represent the Indian spirit at its best.

All Native Americans live in tribal societies. The word Seminole is a Miccosukee word meaning "wild" or "runaway" and pertains to the renegade who fled native homelands for America's southernmost state. Out of this fabric, the Seminole nation began.

From this dramatic beginning, baby James grew under his grandparents' nurturing. His grandmother taught him lullabies such as the counting song in his native tongue. From birth, Chief Billie could talk with the other inhabitants of the Everglades, whether they were man or animal. His grandmother used to rock him to sleep and hold him next to her heart. Her love for him translated into the rhythmic beat of her heart as he lay snuggled in her arms. Her song taught him to count from one to ten in Seminole.

"I keep my enemies nearby where I can watch them,"

said Chief Billie to his long-time white friend who he jokingly calls Tonto. He is aware of everything. He examines the height of spider webs to see if the children have been around. Preferring to go barefoot, even while hunting, Chief Billie has the area around his chickee swept so he can see whose footprints are outside. Then he knows whether his enemies have been listening to his private talks.

"To the Indians," says Tonto of his sidekick, "Chief Billie is the equivalent of the President of the United States. When he goes hunting, James Billie can catch fish with his bare hands. He can also catch animals that way. It's remarkable to watch him. He just knows."

This quality of knowingness comes from his harmony with his environment. It is not a quality that can be learned from books, but rather an initiation into the rites of the Indian. This knowledge is more akin to that of the Ninja warrior who fought with his secret form of body energy and his own weapons. Chief Billie uses all his senses to blend his energy with that of the universe. It has stood him in good stead.

His son's name Micco is Indian for "leader of the town," or "King." This position was occasionally hereditary, although the chief could be impeached and removed by the council under Creek law. In some tribes one clan was the ruling clan and the micco always came from this clan. This tradition is not true of the Seminoles of Florida. They have elected chiefs from different clans.

James encourages his tribal members to reach their full potential. He flies a jet plane to show everyone that they can have whatever they want in life.

The Seminole Tribe of Florida's Christmas party was held at the Broward Convention Center. There were approximately 3,000 people there, mostly tribal members, including a one month old baby. There were so many people there that there wasn't room for the dessert table, which had to be located outside the room in the lobby.

At the party, James was dressed in a tuxedo and acted as the master of ceremonies. It was a gala affair, with a buffet dinner consisting of prime rib and many other dishes, although iced tea was served instead of alcoholic drinks. On stage, two huge screens at both ends of the room showed the action on stage, slides of tribal members, and the concert featuring John Anderson, who had the number one country music video and whose song *Seminole Wind* was on the top of the country charts. He was inspired to write the song while visiting the Seminole reservation of Big Cypress.

Chief Billie wanted to give his grandmother and grandfather a present. Robb Tiller had a Mercedes which he sold to James for $5,000. James hired a white chauffeur named Irvin to take them around the reservation.

His grandparents loved riding around wherever they wanted to go. They went to visit friends and relatives on other reservations. They went to the Seminole Fair in Hollywood.

But the car began to overheat. They decided they had done enough traveling. James gave the car to two old women who needed transportation. A few days later, he saw the women walking.

"What happened to the Mercedes I gave you?" asked James curiously.

"It's back there," replied the women. The car had self-destructed. All the engine parts had fallen out on the ground, leaving a trail of metal along the road.

Whatever mixed heritage Seminoles have, James Billie wants them to have a secure future with capitalism. The clan structure helped the Seminoles keep track of their heritage with living individuals, but once a clan member died, his genealogy became clouded. Just as the black slaves had trouble tracing their ancestry, the Native American's ways were continually being disrupted by the white settlers and the white soldiers.

Thrown into this ring to further complicate the issue is the mixed heritage of many present-day Native Americans.

As a young man, James felt at home with the Turners. James called them Mom and Dad and ate with their children. He became part of their family. Naturally, the subject of adoption was raised. Since James was half Seminole, the adoption had to be approved by the Tribal Council.

When Pete went before the Tribal Council in 1959, he asked permission to adopt James.

"Mr. Tiger, who was a member of the council, explained that if adoption occurred, James would lose all his rights as an Indian. Now I was not going to jeopardize anything he could have as an Indian. Also, we served beer at the restaurant my wife ran, so they raised that as an issue. I decided that I didn't want to take anything away from James that he was entitled to from the Seminoles," Pete said.

"I said I wanted to see some strong efforts from the tribe to take care of him," said Pete.

"Our biggest contribution to his advancement was that he continue his Indian heritage and not give it up," observed Pete.

34

"He still calls me up to ask me about a Lycoming aircraft engine that wouldn't run right on his black airboat. Water had gotten into his carburetor. His engine would fire and then die. He had to change both the filter and carburetor because the water blocks the jets."

This ability to draw talented people to him like a magnet would cement the young James' future success. An Indian with Indians, James could also easily interact and charm the white community at a very young age.

There were many men in the business community who flew as naval pilots in the service. James encountered Bill Bennett, chairman of the board of Circus Circus, the big casino corporation in Las Vegas. When Bill was asked about possible parentage, he replied humorously, "As wild as I was when I was a naval pilot, it is perfectly possible I'm James' father. If so, I pray I never find out."

The chief answered, "Bill can stop praying because he's too young to be my father, but it's possible he's my long lost brother."

Chief Billie's roots can never be completely known. His tribesmen provided for him because he is a member of the Bird clan. As chief of the Seminole Tribe of Florida, his responsibility is to lead the tribe as fearlessly and competently as his ancestors did.

Seminole girl with baby

Chapter 4

Reconnaissance in Vietnam

*I*nspired by the example of the father he never knew, James served two tours of duty in Vietnam, beginning in 1966.

"We were regular army," explained James about Vietnam. "We enlisted. My squad and I wanted to be there. We had a better attitude and a better success rate than the other guys that got drafted. They'd sit around and complain about being there. We thought about it like we were hired to do the job."

James served with a tough crew of macho men. Some of his fellow soldiers were trying to obtain American citizenship. There were men from the Bahamas and Mexico who wanted United States papers. There was a guy James remembers whose motorcycle had been confiscated so he decided to enlist.

The battlefield was more familiar to a tough Seminole raised in the Everglades than it was to a street kid from New Jersey. Some of the city kids were at a real disadvantage. James was assigned to long-range reconnaissance. He was cross trained in all kinds of vehicles. One of his jobs was to drive a tank. It was not the kind you operate with pedals, but all automatic.

On one of his assignments, the unit he was commanding was below Da Nang in Si Winn in Ny Trang and Cameron Bay. It was July. Their platoon's orders were to observe the valley below from their mountaintop camp. One hot meal a day was delivered to them by helicopter.

"Tarzan was my hero as a boy," relates Chief Billie. "I used to listen to him on the radio along with Hopalong Cassidy and the others. I always wondered how he could do what he did in the jungle."

When he was first shipped to Vietnam, Private James Billie drew on his boyhood experiences in the woods. His grandfather used to give him a shotgun with only one shell in it.

"Make sure you know what you're shooting. If you can't hit it, don't shoot at it," were the words his grandfather had said to him. Since his aim in those days determined what they had for supper, he learned to be an expert shot.

He was shipped out with Charlie company, 23rd Infantry, then switched to the 101st Infantry. He began with a machine outfit with the 25th. His assignment was on alpha squad in charge of perimeter watch.

The orders from Sergeant Chahooe were to do what you learned in basic training. "Anything that comes down this trail is the enemy." Standing watch was tiring. The first time he was alone, James was nervous. Behind him, he heard some chatter that sounded like "Hey you." When he turned around to check, it turned out to be only a gecko lizard sunning on a rock.

Up in the mountains, Private Billie got a kind of vertigo. After a long time, here came a soldier. He took the safety off his M16 rifle. He was 100 yards away. He knew that he could hit him easily from here, but the words of his grandfather rang in his ears. He put his gun down to wait.

"I must have picked up and put down my rifle 20 times. If it hadn't been for the advice of my grandfather, I would have killed him. I knew I could do it with the M16. Then it dawned on me—I had let him get closer and closer—finally I could see his uniform. It was my relief coming!" If James had shot him, he could have been court-marshaled. It would have changed his life forever.

"Those words of my grandfather's saved me. My grandfather always said be sure you know what you're shooting.

"Some of the men who came back from Vietnam died over here," added the veteran. "They didn't have any more battles to fight or a tribe to care for them like I did with the Seminoles. Soldiers are best when they have a battle to fight."

Chief Billie has been guided by *The Prince* by Machiavelli and *The Art of War* which explains how crucial it is to get troops to the scene of battle as quickly as possible.

He believes every American should be entitled to carry a gun to defend himself. He states that the National Rifleman's Association is right about this point.

"Someone could come to my house and if they didn't come in my door, I could be lying down dead and they'd never know it. In the old days, people were closer. If I had food, I'd share it with the rest." Chief Billie is very generous in buying dinner for his friends and tribesmen.

"I'd like to go down to South America to an Indian village where rural people care for each other. If I spoke Spanish, I'd go there looking for wisdom," said the Chief. "I want to know the spectrum."

In the book, *The Art of War,* the many problems of warfare are addressed. One strategy was to get the troops to the front line quickly. Since the leaders didn't have airplanes, they had to march the soldiers into battle.

"In those days, war was very spread out. That made it expensive to move troops. Sometimes they would have to cover hundreds of miles on foot," James pointed out. "I used to put smoke on me before going into battle for protection like my grandfather taught me. My division got so they'd ask me to bless them with it too. They'd say, 'Do you have a cigarette, sergeant?' I'd wave my cigarette in front of them. I'd know what they were asking." Smoke was a part of the Seminole ritual that Chief Billie carried with him to Vietnam. Vietnam gave James the opportunity to apply his Seminole reconnaissance skills to jungle warfare. He knew the importance of healing from the shaman of his tribe. In his unit there were Mormons, many of whom were conscientious objectors. They usually had to ship them to other squads, but there was one who James recognized would make a fine medic. This soldier would crawl out on the front lines and administer to the sick.

War was yet another training ground for James on his journey towards tribal leadership. He approached every situation cautiously and was ready for any emergency.

Once James and his platoon were going down a river near Cambodia. They saw this wave coming towards them. It was a twenty-foot anaconda swimming down the river. The snake is a constrictor, like a python.

"We got out of the river as fast as we could," said James. "We weren't worried about the Vietcong when we saw the size of that anaconda."

James and his platoon marched out into the jungle. He was carrying his radio; inside the radio case was his lunch. He reached inside the case, pulled out his provisions, and ate them. Then he stuffed the remains back under the cover. When he got back to where they were setting up perimeter watch for the night, he pulled out his food. Inside the radio case was a bamboo rattlesnake.

"Everyone around me started shaking out their bags," said James.

In a letter to General Clinch in 1836, the war Chief Osceola said, "You have guns and so do we; you have powder and lead and so do we; you have men and so have we; your men will fight and so will ours, until the last drop of the Seminoles' blood has moistened the dust of his hunting grounds."

James' grandfather taught him reconnaissance when he was a little boy. They would go out and see where the food that the deer liked grew. Then, when they returned to that spot, they found the deer.

The lessons James learned from his Seminole grandfather were valuable in the hills and rivers of Vietnam. His training as a youth gave him an advantage in the battlefields where mistakes were very costly.

Chief Billie finds a serenity at Big Cypress reservation, which is in the woods, surrounded by swamp. Once he was given a trip to New York City. He had a suite at the Waldorf Astoria Hotel overlooking Central Park. He decided a walk through Central Park would be relaxing because there would be birds around like there were back at Big Cypress. When he strolled along, he encountered a very different kind of bird than those back in the Everglades.

In contrast to the New York experience, James liked the country when he was in Vietnam because it was reminiscent of the swamp where he had hunted and fished. In war he became a crack soldier, partly because he was determined to follow in the footsteps of his father, and partly because of his extraordinary ability to size up a situation instantly.

"I wanted to learn to fly because my father was a naval pilot," says James. "And I wanted to go to war because he did."

He is concerned that the tribe is forgetting the old ways. The older members were more self-sufficient. After the tribe became organized, "we became like that domestic alligator—always waiting for handouts. The wild alligator got skinny when it was bad and got fat when it was good."

James had a friend in Vietnam that he nicknamed Warmonger, because the guy liked to kill. As he was about to be discharged, the soldier volunteered for a final mission where he was killed by the Vietcong.

As a point man on reconnaissance, James worked alone. He liked to move early in the morning because the dew would cling to the trip wires and they would be visible.

When his turn for R and R came up, he had to leave immediately. He left for Taiwan. When he returned, he asked about his squad.

"They're all dead," was the reply he received. His replacement had taken them down the same trail that James had led them up the previous week.

"You never use the same trail," said James. "They were suffocated with their heads stuck in the sand until they turned blue."

After fourteen months in Vietnam, James contracted malaria and was sent to the hospital. There he was visited by Connie Francis and Raymond Burr.

When he returned from the war, he stayed in Moore Haven for awhile with Pete and Nina Turner, the white people who had wanted to adopt him as a child. He slept in the pine trees behind their house. When it rained he came inside.

Nina offered him their couch, but he refused.

"I'm an Indian. I'll sleep on the floor," said James.

James had a very important job in Vietnam. He would have to find groups of the enemy and not get caught.

"It was impossible for anyone else but James to do that," explained Pete Turner, a fighter pilot in World War II. "He sometimes had to kill the enemy quietly. He would call in on the radio and report what he found in code."

Spiderwebs along the trail meant that no one had walked there during the night. Downplaying the dangers, James explained that actually it wasn't very different from the Everglades, except there were rice patties in Vietnam instead of alligators.

In World War I, Indians in the American and Canadian forces had sent messages in their native tongues. Their vocabulary was limited, however, because they lacked words for the armaments of combat.

In World War II, the Navajo Indians used the Navajo language to communicate privately amongst themselves. Known secretly as the "Code Talkers," the Navajos devised an oral communication that could not be broken by Naval Intelligence officers because the language roots are tonal, based as they are on Athabaskan tongues brought from Asia. Tonal languages have different meanings for different ways the same word is pronounced.

After 1940, the Japanese "Purple Code" was broken. Intercepted Japanese messages were subjected to a decoding cryptographic device, code-named "Magic," a process which required several hours.

However, the Navajo code was never broken. The Navajos sent their coded messages instantly and they were just as quickly decoded by a receiving Navajo trained in the code. The advantages of Indian codes, besides the obvious language difficulty, is the Native American training to keep everything in memory.

From the Seminole counting song that James learned at birth, to the hunting prayer taught to him by his grandfather, all the lessons of his life James committed to memory. It would have been easy to train him to use Seminole to deceive the Vietcong during his reconnaissance trips.

"James asked me why I didn't own an airplane after the war," said Pete Turner, a World War II Army pilot. "I said I couldn't afford one because I was working as a mechanic and wasn't making enough money. 'Don't buy an airplane unless you can afford one,' I told him. James went on to make several million dollars," said Pete.

Chapter 5

The Power of Shamanism

As a Seminole, James Billie was taught shamanistic powers from boyhood. An Indian shaman is indoctrinated into the practice and can choose what path he wants to take with his life. Chief Billie's goals were three: to have good health, to have a smile on his face, and to have a guitar in his hands. At his ceremony, he had a bucket of water to baptize himself. He took the cold water and poured it all over his head. The cold shock caused his face to scrunch up in a grimace! Regarding his guitar, he says jokingly that he asked for a guitar in his hands, but "I wish I had said I wanted to be able to play it!"

James believes in miracles. He also believes in dreams. He is wary of organized religion like the Baptist faith he encountered as a child. He has his own form of Indian religion. He is not an atheist.

Each shaman has his own art of healing. Most want to purify themselves. Some can predict hurricanes. Seminole shaman were looking towards the sky to give weather forecasts long before there were meteorologists. A shaman can not only consult the different elements, but can also use his power for hindrance or for good. If Chief

Billie sees something dying off, he just thinks it's meant to be that way. He believes that the Creator made things on this earth in order for them to survive, not in perpetual harmony, but in active relationships that can even be cannibalistic.

Anthropologists agree that all societies have one thing in common—a belief in a great spirit or higher power. In order to exert some control over their environment, a group or tribe exhorts this greater being through dances, prayers, sacrifices or songs. The Seminoles call their God "The Breath Maker."

Different Seminole shamans have different talents. Making rain is a specialty of Bobby Henry, an independent Seminole from Tampa. Called upon by desperate public officials, Henry has performed his ritualistic dance and ceremony to end severe droughts. Rain has come shortly after his supplications. As with our medical doctors, some shaman specialize in diagnosing diseases, while others attempt to remedy them. They learn their techniques through long apprenticeships under more experienced shaman and hand down the knowledge to younger generations.

A shaman must be spiritually attuned. His special medicine pouch contains herbs, animal horns, roots and other natural ingredients. He goes through an eight year study to attain his rank.

Seminole tribes have rituals for their dead, just as most societies do. Traditional technique left the body on an open platform guarded by someone such as a slave so that animals wouldn't steal it. It would have been difficult to bury bodies below the earth in the Everglades because of the high water table.

Seminoles around a smoky campfire.
Chief Billie with his knife at the ready.

When a Seminole dies, their family mourns for four days and on the fourth morning they use herbs that the medicine man gives them. They will drink them with tea Or wash with them. The wife wears black and mourns for four moons—it is part of tradition.

Tribal medicine rites remain a mystery. Protected by the initiated, the practices are guarded by the Seminoles who have handed down the secrets from generation to generation. Outsiders are left to speculate on the ancient rituals that many believe assured the tribe's survival.

As with the clans, animals provided a totemic belief. A warrior could take on the cunning of a panther if he killed one. A hunter could be fleet as a deer if he ate deer meat.

Seminole shamans call upon their spiritual powers once a year at the Green Corn Dance in early summer to help the tribes achieve their objectives—be it war, a good harvest, or a wet growing season. Native American's desire to control his environment in the areas of fertility, harnessing the elements to provide food and shelter, and success in the hunt were all concerns of Seminole medicine.

Tobacco was used by the Seminoles as a spiritual aid in prayer. A medicine pipe was thought to be instrumental in the retrieving the wandering soul by blowing his breath through it. Indians were believed to have two souls. Occasionally, one would leave the body at night and not return unless "his ammunition," or breath, was aimed at it.

Seminole clans each have their own medicine bundle which is kept by the shaman of that clan. The Panther Clan is the medicine keeper of the tribe and is in charge of the main medicine bundle. The medicine bundle is wrapped in deerskin, hair side out, and contains feathers, stones, and other items in buckskin bags. The medicine is so strong that if a woman approached and got too close to it, it would knock her over.

Occasionally the shaman, when called upon to treat a sick or injured Indian, invokes prayer, herbal remedies, and a bit of play-acting. Different operations are performed to cut out the cause of the illness. The shaman palms a stone, a piece of bone, a thorn, or an insect. He then pretends to pull out the offensive item from the open wound. He may place a special black dye in his mouth, then suck some blood from the sore. The dye will mix with the blood, causing it to look black. As he spits it out, the "poison" is removed.

As in many societies, the Seminole shaman must generate belief in his magic powers. Since much of what causes disease is in the mind, the patient's belief in the shaman's ability to heal is essential. Every Indian tribe needs to know that they have a shaman who is powerful enough to combat any health problem. Experience has taught Indians that they will encounter many such problems and their shaman is the healer they can count on.

The shaman are not only consulted for physical ailments, but also for mental ones, such as bad dreams, harsh misfortunes, and sexual failures. Shaman are versed in changing the weather and can guarantee better hunting. With each foray into battle, the shaman is close by to administer to the wounded. Hunts begin with an incantation by the shaman to assure a safe return. Everything needed for the Seminoles' well-being is available from the shaman. Each tribal council consists of one shaman and two or three council members.

Indians believed they lived in an orderly universe where nature was delicately balanced and could be easily upset. They themselves upset nature when they hunted and killed animals. Therefore, they apologized to the animals ritually and purified themselves by sweating and bathing after the hunt. These actions kept nature pacified, but if they were overlooked, the animals were angered and sent disease and discomfort to them.

When Josie Billie, the principal shaman since 1937 of the Trail Seminoles, became a practicing Baptist, he turned over possession of the medicine bundle to his brother Ingraham Billie. Ingraham Billie has taught both Joel Frank and Chief Billie some of the secrets of the Seminole shaman.

Shamans deserved a certain amount of respect because they were believed to be imbued with supernatural powers. These powers could be used against an Indian if he misbehaved. The Indians believed that disaster would result if the shaman was defied.

"As part of the present day training, the initiate must make several journeys into the woods alone," Chief Billie says.

"You've got to do things the old-fashioned way. You all the chants and sing songs and do things that are not written down," Billie says. "Vines, stumps, logs—all the necessities and all that make life miserable are there, yet we go into it to etch out a little place to survive four days of fasting. During that time you find yourself, your animal self, or your animal spirit guide."

Practical knowledge of healing for bruises, sprains, and broken bones was in the shaman's bailiwick. In public ceremonies, the shaman had to display his expertise.

A student can study on his own, but must return on the first month of the year to gain further instruction and to get help with his training. He must learn chants and songs. In order to cure, one must learn the proper magical chants and formulas. Hence, the teaching of the songs in connection with each one of the various types of disease forms a significant part of the training of a new medicine man.

Fortunately, these Seminoles will carry forward the tradition of the shaman so that future generations will be able to preserve the ancient customs of the healer. It is only through their study and attainment that the shaman will not disappear like some clans that have died out within the Seminole tribe.

Shaman are responsible for keeping order. For example, if someone eats an animal that is deemed inedible, such as a snake or a bat, that person must be cleaned out with the herbal potion known as "the black drink." This is administered to make the person vomit, thereby cleansing him. Other taboo areas are corrected, but individuals are ultimately in charge of their own destiny. Shaman, along with the elders in the clan, make sure men take care of their children, even if they are divorced and living at a new wife's house. A woman may indicate she wants a husband out by placing his clothes and tools on the doorstep. A man can become divorced just by walking out. Presumably, the shaman is not a marriage counselor, as he doesn't need to be.

Shaman Josie Billie was one of James's teachers. The shaman presided at the annual Green Corn Dance in the summer and the Hunting Dance in the fall. He was consulted whenever there was a judgment to make.

As in other areas of Seminole life, the old and the new are merging in medicine. Federal contracts provide doctors and dentists. If a doctor works on an Indian reservation after graduation, his medical school tuition is paid by the federal government. Modern medicines, such as Epsom salts, rubbing alcohol and other prepared drugs, were allowed because Josie Billie referred Seminoles to white doctors.

After the Turners attempted to adopt James, he went back the Hollywood reservation to live with Laura Mae and Max Osceola. When James first came to live with the Osceolas he didn't know how old he was or what birthdays were. He had never celebrated one before.

"I'm not a person that sits quiet," said Laura Mae Osceola. She was a close friend of Agnes Billie because they attended the Cherokee boarding school together when they were growing up. Laura Mae was born on November 13, 1932, her "good luck" day.

Laura Mae remembers James had a pet raccoon named Bugger. "We had so many problems with him. We'd leave him in and he'd get out. If we tied him to a tree, he'd break his leash. We'd have to chase him all over. He'd be in the neighbor's yard and we'd have to get him back."

"Tommie was born out of incest, so the family didn't care for her. She was a misfit. They travelled a lot and kept moving around. My stepfather was a member of the Bird Clan. He said she was a human being and had to be treated with respect."

"Before James was born we used to stay with my mother, Kathy Tommie Jumper Smith, and Morgan Smith, her second husband, during the Green Corn Dance at Big Cypress. Tommie was given to an old man. At first, we all thought Agnes was their child, but that is now disputed. Frank Billie is admitting he's James' uncle, so now we don't think his grandfather was the old man. He was Jimmie Billie that died in Rayeford. Everybody loves James now because he's the tribal chairman.

"The young boys kept fooling with Tommie. Now we think Josie Billie, the shaman, is James' grandfather. My mother knew James' grandfather from Miami. He was kin to Morgan Smith. Tommie came to live with and marry John Billie. When he got drunk he was a terror. The two misfits got together. John Billie hit and pushed around two pregnant women. Tommie and John lived in Mesail Village, one of the commercial tourist camps.

"The old man was crippled. He said, 'I'll have to take care of the problem.' So someone drove him in a truck to the village. John was a good mechanic. They called to him to come out and fix the truck. He was helping cook breakfast. The old man shot and killed him because the two girls were kin to him. Then she travelled to Hollywood. We didn't criticize much around here.

"Tommie then married Frank Tommie, who introduced her to Delray. After that, she married John Buster from Big Cypress who used to hunt there. She moved up there with Agnes and Annie. The girls were interested in going away school during World War II.

"There was a Naval base located in Davie. It was part of the Bermuda triangle. George Bush who later became US president was stationed there. The navy men drove their liberty truck along Sterling Road. The girls were going to the movies. They would get a ride to Hollywood on that liberty truck. Wartime was a time when the whites and the Seminoles intermingled.

"Agnes and I were good friends. She was older than me. We would spend the night together. Frank Tommie was my uncle and I liked the family.

"Agnes ran around that summer with J. W. Barnett. She didn't know she was pregnant. 'I'm not eating a lot, but I'm getting big,' she confided to me.

At the Christmas holiday, Betty Mae brought her back to Hollywood. Laura Mae cried and cried because she had to leave.

"She asked me if I had a half-white baby, what would I do? I told her I'd keep him. I was crying. She had her baby at the Chimpanzee Farm in Dania. Betty Mae Jumper's mother delivered him.

"She made me promise that if anything happened to her, because the Indian people didn't like her, she said to

53

me, 'I want you to take that baby.' I said I would."

"Laura Mae used to babysit at night and James used to sleep between the girls. Then she'd go back to school with him before she married when James was 6 or 7.

"My mother Kathy, and stepfather Morgan Smith, taught James to do cows. My mother drank when she was a young lady so they got to be good friends way before James was born. She used to visit and they would leave him with us.

"I got married and moved to Hollywood with Max. Then Annie married a Cherokee, named Richard Wolf. That left Grandma alone. Sometimes she'd have to go to Miami. Then she'd leave James with Tommie Billie, his grandmother. Sonnie Billie then married Agnes Billie, James' mother. He was a shaman living at Big Cypress. After she died of a heart problem, I wanted to take Charles, too. I was supposed to take care of her kids. I figured Charles had a father and when Agnes died, the father wanted him. Charles grew up with a white family.

"Finally we lived in a one room house near 441. It used to have French windows. We were the first family to have a TV. My son, Max, was about 4 or 5 and he used to go down to the grocery store. James had not visited us for a long time. I can see him hanging on the two French doors, barefoot, his seat dirty, in cutoffs with long hair. We came around the corner. He'd take off like a scared rabbit. I still worried about him. When he was 11, his grandmother came over and told my husband, a member of the Bird Clan like her: 'I can't control him. I want you to take him. Make him go to school.'

"Max was making good money then, around $66 a week. I had already adopted another little boy. With love you can do things. I was trying to organize the tribe in 1953. I went up to Washington, D. C. in 1953 on the termination of the tribes. We were organizing in 1957.

"James' stepfather was afraid for him to be with white people. We got him in the 50's. During that time he had been doing what he wanted to do.

"We all used to go riding on Sunday. We would drive to Miami to the car races or to see the flamingoes. We would go to the Tamiami Trail. To get to my mother's we'd drive up to Clewiston on US Route 27. I'd pack some sandwiches and Coke and we'd have a picnic.

"I had to go somewhere. I asked Willie Tiger, one of the elders, to keep him. I gave him some grocery money and told him to get more food on credit and I'll come back and pay you. The food was gone. He stole some food. I said it wasn't right to do that. That wasn't the Indian way. He wanted to go with Morgan. He ran away to Morgan.

"They liked him, so he went hunting with them. I told him that they were his Tarzan days. He attended Haskell Junior High School in Lawrence, Kansas. He graduated from Clewiston, then went to college in Lake City for a while, then joined the army.

Max and Laura Mae divorced. James stayed in Laura Mae's house and went to school.

"I used to say I borned him. He was trained very religiously. I spanked him when he was 16 years old. His brothers were Max, Jr., and Lawrence. Sharon was his sister in adoption.

"I was like a mother hen. Nobody fooled with my kids. I had bought Max and James shoes. Allen Jumper took his shoes and threw them into the telephone wires.

55

That was the first time I be angry. They called him a white boy. I told him everyday that he was just as good as anybody else. There are famous people on your white side and famous people on your Indian side.

"He had some insecurity. I still see it creep out. I cut his hair. He was one of my own. I try to stay away from him now. I see so many people bothering him.

"I still give him advice. Sometimes what I say comes right. It's because I love him.

"James was a lady's man when he was little. He'd be at the Brighton church meetings and all the girls would surround him. He'd tell stories. Sometimes I'd get after him. I ran that house like a ship. I'd be working in the office. I left a note on the refrigerator. They had chores to do. After they got finished, they could go to the rec hall for about half an hour. The chores took them awhile.

"They could have a moon pie for a snack. Then they went down to the gym. Be back when I got home, I'd say.

"Now I have a granddaughter, Melissa. She's sixteen. She'll tell me, 'Grandma, I'm so tired. I'm worn out.' This summer James sent her to Paris. She's my son Max's daughter. What are you doing to her? I ask Max. She brought James a bottle of wine from France.

"Max answered, 'You used to be hard on us.' I kept them busy when they were that age.

"We'd go to the Southern Baptist church where Reverend Genus Crenshaw preached. He and his wife, Carolyn, have been here in Hollywood for the past 35 years. They knew James' grandmother well."

The Seminole Tribe of Florida is a close-knit group of Indians. The shamanistic ways of the Seminoles kept the men and women together in a spiritual way at times when they were separated physically from nurturing family ties. In this way James' shaman training was valuable preparation for what was to be a challenging future for the chief.

Frank Weed and James hold panther cub.

Chapter 6

The Jim Billie Show

James taught himself to play the guitar when he was 12. His grandmother sung him Seminole legends that he wanted to set to music. James' love of music began to flourish. He'd sit in Laura Mae Osceola's kitchen and sing and sing.

"Mom, help me translate this song," James would ask her.

He was trying to put the lyrics of the song *Summertime* in Seminole with the music. The words are different lengths. Summer is "la-catse." Living is a long word in Seminole. He was having a challenging time doing it.

James has made several tapes of his songs. His CD *Native Son* has been released through **Tomorrow's Stars** recording company. His guitar is his instrument of expression as well as an accompaniment to the songs James remembers from his childhood. He has also composed and written his own original melodies.

James has entertained in many clubs around Florida, including Citrus Towers in Orlando, Sportsman's Paradise in Moore Haven, and The Calusa Lodge in Lakeport. He appeared at the Grand Ole Opry in Nashville, Tennessee. His singing is rich and full of animal imagery like his stories. He also writes songs about great Seminoles, such as a recent song about Josie Billie, the medicine man. James has several guitars strewn around his house. He is constantly perfecting his tunes and lyrics. He carries his guitar in his truck and performs in local restaurants.

James attended the Florida Folk Festival in White Springs in 1978, where the participants camped, jammed and exchanged stories. James met other guitarists, folklorists and fiddlers there. One of the participants, Pat Wickman, became a friend of Chief Billie.

James has a massive amount of drive and imagination. Life tends to move and shake when he's projecting what to do next. He can think bigger and better than most people. He doesn't care how long it takes to bring ideas to fruition, the sign of a true visionary.

Pat terms herself "an adventure junkie." As a historian, her life isn't made up of security and peace and quiet. She has known James for 15 years. A visit to Big Cypress Reservation for her is like a ride on Space Mountain—a high speed, high turbulence ride. Pat, a guitarist like James, knew Will McClellan, the black hat troubadour who attended the Steven Foster Memorial Folk Festival with James. James still enjoys singing Will's songs.

James dares to do everything. He encouraged Pat to complete her book on a Seminole war chief "Osceola's Legacy" published by the University of Alabama Press. He sees no limits and expects those around him to reach higher and higher.

"When I was escorting a group of Spanish visitors and interpreting for them, James sunk down in a chair next to me and confided, 'Sometimes I feel like I'm walking around in a whirlwind,'" said Pat.

James is constantly improvising lyrics. He'll work a

song over and over in his head until he gets it finished. His latest song is about mosquitoes, the ever-present insects of the Everglades. He started with an idea. The "skeeter's still here." It developed into a clever tune about "the welcoming committee from Everglades City."

Jay Roberts and James rehearse.

Sometimes he ends up taking flack. When he sang a

61

song about Callijah the wooden Indian, some of the Indians got insulted. He plays around with lyrics, constantly using humor to charm his audiences. His songs never seem to end. James' mind operates like a computer, processing all the information available, then jumping to conclusions that he'll constantly reevaluate.

"He has his own meter," observed Jay Roberts, a fiddler who plays with James. "He used to be in the audience and asked if he could come up and play with me and my band. We got to be friends. Many musicians who are self-taught do have their own meter."

There were musicians at James' 50th birthday party. He built an auditorium which doubles as a snake show stadium at Billie Swamp Safari. His song is that of the animals and people that inhabit his Everglades world. The swamps that protected the Seminoles from removal and possible oblivion are a place of reverence for James. He will never tire of their hot murky depths as he sings about the tiny red sawgrass flower that blooms there.

James and the fiddler jam together for hours. Jay Roberts has brought along his acoustic drummer and steel drummer for their performance later that evening.

James' musical style is reminiscent of Hoyt Axton, but his lyrics are uniquely his own. He collaborates with other songwriters, gleaning their input, sifting through the verses until he comes up with something that satisfies him.

He discussed the idea for a mosquito song with Norman Monath over the phone. Norman has written hundreds of lyrics for many famous musicians and is the author of many books, including the best seller, *How to Teach Yourself the Guitar in 10 Easy Lessons.*

"He didn't do what I told him to," said James, when he was asked about Norman Monath. James picked out *Danny Boy* from a book of Irish and Scottish folk songs Norman edited as one he liked.

One beautiful Seminole legend that the chief has set to music is a tale of two Indian men who are hunting in the forest. They come upon a log that has two fish in it. One man takes out the fish and prepares them to eat. The other man is afraid to eat the fish. He feels it is unnatural for the fish to be in a log. The man that has eaten the fish is transformed into a snake. His body forms the Kissimmee River which runs into Lake Okeechobee where he lives. When his relatives come to fish, they see him but don't recognize him in a snake's body. He scares them away by talking to them. Then he leaves through the Caloosahatchee River and runs away into the Gulf of Mexico.

James's son Micco loves to imitate his father. James was strumming his guitar in the buff one morning. Micco spied him and started pulling off his shirt. Leslie helped him get it off. Then he went "Mmm, mm," to his diaper. That came off as well. Micco got his toy guitar. There they sat, the chief with his son, nakedly playing their guitars. Micco smiled proudly at his mother.

"Sometimes I think I play backdrop to my son," admits James, who is a very doting father. When Leslie suggested that the housekeeper wanted to have Micco stay with her on a recent trip to the Cayman Islands, James answered "over my dead body."

James readily admits he's a showman. He's lived around tourist attractions all his life. A favorite hat of his is sewn together with thread where an alligator bit through it.

"This hat saved my butt," says the chief proudly. He was wrestling alligators and one got too close for comfort.

Some of the music reflects pain. "Warmonger" is a song about his good friend in Vietnam who went out on one last voluntary mission and never returned. He has lost many friends and relatives, most recently, Max Osceola, his adopted father. Max was killed in a car crash in Hollywood.

"I hate to hear the phone ring because I'm afraid it's bad news." James' songs reflect this darker side of life where people die and vanish from his family.

He has survived poisonous snake bites, malaria, the Vietnam war, endangered species trials, the loss of his mother at age nine, the deaths of both grandparents, and the disappointment of never finding his real father. These events have instilled a sadness in his music that in a lesser man could signal his defeat.

Because James is chief of the Seminoles, he has an image to uphold. He takes this role very seriously. His leadership of a tribe of 2,000 will determine how success-ful these proud Native Americans are in marking out each tribal member's future.

James is so caught up in the decision-making of day-to-day events, he uses his music as a way to relax and get away from the stress of charting the political course in many economic enterprises.

Once he was picking up his new golden lab puppy. As he was about to enter the house, the owner warned everyone that there might be something that will jump out.

"Like what?" asked James, guarding against the improbable, his mind full of many alternatives. It was just the bouncing yellow puppy this time.

He has made four videos in addition to his CDs and tapes. *Native Son* is one he made with his wife Bobbi. *The Path to Self Reliance* is in an informational tone. *The Way of the Glades* is a breathtaking look at the deer and panther in the Everglades. An alligator video is his latest.

A Seminole shaman remembers his medicine through Indian chants. Music permeates their culture—be it the Indian counting song that women sing to their babies, or the shake of tortoise shell rattles used to celebrate the annual Green Corn Dances held every year on the five reservations. Native Americans are attuned to the songs of their heritage in a spiritual way, in the same way gospel singers belt out their religion. James enjoys sharing his songs with friends and audiences.

He gives concerts all over Florida. Ticketmaster carries his schedule so that seats are available to his many fans. A recent event was held at the Tierra Verde Resort in St. Petersburg. Billed as the "Jim Billie Show," he entertained the audience with his songs and stories. He played with the lead guitarist from a band called "Big Dick and the Extenders" who played on Duck Key and at the Lorilei Club in Islamorada. Harry French opened for them.

"Don't wait too long," is one of James' favorite sayings. He is impatient to get where he wants to be in of all his endeavors.

He is fast becoming a major star in the country music field. He is well-versed in all kinds of music as evidenced by his greeting me by singing "Barbara-Ann, Barbara-Ann."

The chief gives many of the people he meets nicknames or Indian names. He calls Dr. Jim Fatigan "Skinny-again." It is his way of making new people a part of his family.

Robb Tiller, whose Indian name was given to him in jest by Chief Billie as Chief Walking Eagle "because he's so full of shit he can't fly," remembers when a hungry alligator snatched a yellow lab. The dog belonged to Chief Billie and was identical to Robb's golden lab, "Puppy."

"The alligator swallowed the lab. James stuck his hand into the gator's mouth and pulled out the dog, but it was too late. The dog was already dead," said Robb, who gave Chief Billie another yellow lab named "Bingo" as a gift.

"Big Alligator" is the title of the song on the album *Native Son* that tells this story. The lyrics go:

> **Big alligator, he's mysterious**
> **Big alligator, he's amphibious**
> **Big alligator, he's dangerous**
> **But, with a big alligator you can be prosperous.**
>
> **I was raised in the swamp by my old grandma**
> **We ate turtle meat, a fish called gar**
> **Grandpa told me about panthers and bear**
> **But most of all he told me to beware:**
>
> > **Of hul-pah-te cho-bee**
> > > **Nock-sho-nitch-kee-kah**
> > **Hul-pah-te cho-bee**
> > > **Oo-kun kay-ye-wah**
> > **Hul-pah-te cho-bee**
> > > **Hen-nu-kah che-che-wah**
>
> **As the days of summer grew longer and hot**
> **Grandpa took me on my first gator hunt**
> **We pushed through sawgrass and willow sloughs**
> **With a yellow-eyed dog in a dugout canoe**

66

The dog started sniffin', somethin' in the air
Grandpa said, "Must be gator over there.
Better grab your knife and some rope.
Remember what I told you when you was a boy:"

About hul-pah-te cho-bee
Nock-sho-nitch-kee-kah
Hul-pah-te cho-bee
Oo-kun kay-ye-wah
Hul-pah-te cho-bee
Hen-nu-kah che-che-wah
Hul-pah-te cho-bee
He-mah-shah che-wah

At the age of twelve, I was sure of myself
I could catch alligators by myself
But my dog didn't know what my grandpa said
He jumped in the water by the gator's head
Hul-pah-te-cho-bee didn't even pause
My dog disappeared in the gator's jaws
I can still hear my grandpa saying:

Hul-pah-te cho-bee
Nock-sho-nitch-kee-kah
Hul-pah-te cho-bee
Oo-kun kay-ye-wah
Hul-pah-te cho-bee
He-mah-shah che-wah

Oh, hul-pah-te cho-bee
Nock-sho-nitch-kee-kah
Hul-pah-te cho-bee
Oo-kun kay-ye-wah
Hul-pah-te cho-bee
Hen-nu-kah che-che-wah
Hul-pah-te cho-bee
He-mah-shah che-wah

Many years later I remembered that day
How that big bull gator swallowed my dog
Scars and pain haunts my life
But I've learned to live and I've learned to survive

With hul-pah-te cho-bee
    Nock-sho-nitch-kee-kah
Hul-pah-te cho-bee
    Ob-kun kay-ye-wah
Hul-pah-te cho-bee
    Hen-nu-kah che-che-wah
Hul-pah-te cho-bee
    He-mah-shah che-wah
Oh, hul-pah-te cho-bee
    Nock-sho-nitch-kee-kah
Hul-pah-te cho-bee
    Oo-kuh kay-ye-wah
Hul-pah-te cho-bee
    He-mah-shah che-wah
Hul-pah-te cho-bee
    Hul-pah-te cho-bee.

There are many different themes to Chief Billie's songs. He sings Seminole legends that he has adapted to music. The tunes he plays on his guitar and sings are constantly changing. Some are sad, some are funny, and others have a message for young people.

One of these with a message is *Try and Try Again.* The lyrics go like this:

Little boy walking with his britches rolled up
    And a cane pole in his hand
You know he's mad, but he's not sad
    Cause he lost that big one today

A day will come when he catches that one
　　That somehow got away
He knows by now you never quit
　　You try and try again
(chorus)

And the world moves on
　　As it turns it never stops for anyone
You've got to learn how to crawl before you walk
　　Then you run
Remember all those little things that you learned
　　While you're young.

Little boy grows to be a man
　　The challenge is at hand
The going gets tough, life is rough
　　And he doesn't understand

The world he knew as a boy
　　Was never quite this way
Reality he faces now
　　So cold and very cruel

(chorus)

The years go by, he wonders why
　　His luck seems to change
And there's no one to lend a hand
　　When he's down in the drain

But isn't it strange how these things
　　Work out in the end
And all he's got to do

69

> **Is have faith and believe in himself**
> **Again**

(chorus)

> **The young man dreams of saving it all**
> **And how it's going to be**
> **But troubled times have ruined his life**
> **Somehow he can't see**
>
> **But in the dark there's a light**
> **And he finally sees his way**
> **Then he recalls you never quit**
> **You try and try each day.**

(chorus)

A big favorite of Seminole children is the counting song. When James was a child, he would nestle in his grandmother's arms and she would sing him to sleep with this song:

> **Thah me hen, touk lee hen, tou che chen, shee tee tah, chah key paun, e pah pah, ny younsh, kou lee younsh, e yah wounsh, hah pook.**

All these years, he thought it was just a chant. But James' grandmother was teaching him to count from one to ten with a song.

Chapter 7

Alligator Wrestler at Native Village

Before James Billie was elected chief, he merited a reputation as a fearless alligator wrestler. He followed in the footsteps of many other Native Americans who earned their living through work in this traditional form of enterprise—tourism. He constructed a tourist attraction called Native Village on Route 441 in Hollywood across the street from the Hollywood Bingo Hall. It contains a Seminole store that sells craft items and books. In back of it is an animal farm. Maria Califano, the manager, has worked at Native Village for 14 years.

"The impressive thing about James is how he handles alligators. We have an alligator named 'Long Jaws' here that's 12 feet in length. James treats him as though he is a dog. He's brazen and has guts. He's totally fearless. The way he can handle animals is very special. We have panthers, bobcats, fish, snakes, birds, and alligators here," said Maria.

When they were living together, James and Bobbi built the Native Village for their business. Now, after living in Arizona for one and half years, Bobbi has returned to take charge of the operation.

(Rear) Bobbi, James, B.J.
(Front) Shnutchkee and Tommi

"He was her first love," said Maria. "They met and married when they were very young."

As well as animals of all kinds, there is a chickee on display. The tourist attraction sells Native American handiwork. There is also an art gallery that displays the paintings of Guy LeBree who lives on the Peace River, in Arcadia, Florida. He is called "the barefoot artist" because he never wears shoes. His paintings depict environmental scenes of Indians in their natural surroundings.

The Johns own a wonderful painting by Guy LeBree "The Knarled Oak Clan." It is based on a Seminole legend about the little people. The oak tree fills the entire canvas. Bees are coming in and out of the branches. Riding on the bees' backs are Seminole Indian warriors holding bows and arrows. James wants to buy the painting, but the Johns are reluctant to part with it.

The Billies had a glass cage in their house for their wild cats and other wild pets that they couldn't let roam the neighborhood.

The first time James went hunting in Montana, Bobbi accompanied him. She rode along by his side with ice frozen in her hair and on her clothes, looking like a winter princess. For James, the trip has since become an annual event. When their children, Bobbie Jamie, Tommi, and Shnutchkee were growing up, they had a pet lion which James took to school after the principal expressed his disbelief in the pet's existence. The principal changed his mind when James placed the lion on his desk!

Mike and Denise Johns have known James since 1970. Mike, who is known as Skeets, remembers back when Davie had one cop. His grandfather had the first gas station on route 84 when the next traffic light was all the way out to Margate. Skeets is a quarter Choctaw Indian.

73

Wearing a bald-headed Cobra belt that a game commissioner gave him, Skeets has been bitten nine times by poisonous snakes.

(From left) Skeets, Denise, Bobbi and James

James was Skeets and Denise's best man when they got married. They chose a spot in the formal gardens of the Kapok tree. Their wedding date was May 29, 1976.

Davie was the horse capital of the world then. In those days, James drove around in a beat-up Volkswagen with his hair down to his shoulders. Then he was still in a kid stage.

Skeets thinks that the future is going to be aquaculture. He told us that Red Lobster, a restaurant chain specializing in seafood, now gets all their shrimp from Honduras.

The Seminoles had a tradition that they were taught by their elders. If outsiders were told these teachings, they would no longer exist as a people.

One of the main problems of miscommunication occurred at Hollywood, because they were the first to become educated by white men. In our culture, it is proper for the child to look directly at the adult who is addressing him or her. In the Seminole etiquette custom, the Indian child would look away and slightly bow when spoken to by an adult. The teachers didn't understand this difference.

"I'm sure you heard about the Wanna-bes. One time I was called a Wanna-be, " said Denise. "I'm happy being what I am."

Skeets and Denise's children received Indian names from James. Jennifer, 11, is called "yo-lee" meaning Fox. Danny, who at 15 is already trapping alligators, is "kah-hang-gee" which is Miccosukee for Hawk. Jennifer's horse is kept behind their house.

James hires Danny to trap alligators for him. Danny is already an accomplished trapper. Skeets' children also raised a Florida panther in their house.

This feeling that the Seminoles will vanish is common in other tribes throughout the world. Known as the "trail Indians," people living along the road from Miami on Tamiami trail believed that if they learned to write, they'd sign a piece of paper and then be shipped off to Oklahoma. There was a solid basis for believing this because there is also a Seminole Tribe of Oklahoma composed of the Indians forced to relocate there during the Seminole Wars.

"One time Ross and I were in working clothes. We wore our teeth necklaces in those days. James, Ross and I made quite a sight, because Ross walked nice and straight, like an Indian, with a scar running from the middle of his forehead right down his cheek. He took part in the Sioux Sun ceremony where they put bones in your chest and everything. We used to gunfight together. Well, when we walked into the Rustic Inn the whole place got quiet. People stared and stared. James orders blue crabs. He picked up the whole crab and put it in his mouth. As you can imagine, the whole place got quiet again!

"The way we met was that I stopped off at Frank Weeds to drop off some snakes. James called him, looking for someone that works with snakes."

"A lot of bad things happened at Okalee Village. I got a call at 6:30 from the man that came at night. He couldn't find the coyotes or the deer. John met me at the gate.

"'I'll go up around the rodeo grounds,' I said. There was the horse standing still in the middle of the ring. I knew something was wrong. Then I saw the tracks. They were too big to be coyote tracks. They were lion tracks. I started backing up. I saw John. He started running.

James and Ross in Jamaica

"'I think the lions are out. Let's back out of here slowly and see if James has come in.' Luckily, James was in the ticket office.

"'Are you sure? Didn't you go back there?'

"'I'm not going to go back there alone.' When James looked down there, the door to their cage was open. The lions, Cahn and Zulu, had already eaten one guy. James' hair ran up the back of his neck. With his bowlegs, he looked like he stepped out of the caveman period.

"He found the lions under the trees on the other side

77

of the concrete wall. Ross was the owner of the big cats. He had a place in Jamaica. When Castro came in he came over here. 'I'll go and see if I can get them to go back into their cage,' said James.

"He had a club and was jumping up and down yelling. Both lions charged towards James. He must have scared them, because the lions turned away from him. The lions performed a routine where they got up on a circus pedestal for an audience. They were not really trained though. They were dangerous. Ross showed up then. He talked to them and managed to convince them to go back in their cage with a voice command. The lions had eaten the deer. They never did find the coyotes.

"There was another lion incident that I recall. James was at the orientation building. A lion took a little girl into his cage. I was up on top of the 12 foot high fence. I had sent two runners to get him. She was all blue. James ran like he got shot out of a rocket with the keys so we could enter the cage. We entered with a wooden pole. James ran up and hit the lion on the back of his shoulders. The lion showed us his eighth molar. I ran like hell out of the cage. I got a steel pole. James hit the lion so hard that the pole bent over him. I got the rifle. We only had one shell, but James shot the lion dead.

"The girl spent a week in the hospital. She fully recuperated. It was a miracle," said Skeets.

"James and I stayed pretty close even after he became chief. He was getting involved in politics. He and Bobbi had broken down on Hollywood boulevard. I stopped and James invited me to have dinner with them. At that dinner he asked me to take over Native Village for them. This was in 1981. I started working there. He gave the back part to me in 1985. I got the place really fixed up nice with waterfalls, trails, everything. Sometimes tourists would actually get lost in it," Skeets said.

James is a very intelligent man. He's very shrewd. He thinks ahead. If he doesn't like it, he'll tear it down. It used to frustrate the hell out of Skeets. He'll start 15 projects at once. He finishes them all.

They worked together at the Okalee Village at Sterling Road and 441. He made him assistant manager. Skeets was making about $125 a week. They had a chickee construction business.

"I said to James, 'you should run for chief.' He replied, 'Me? Chief?'

"The next thing I knew, he asked if I could run the village for him for a year. He was going to start his campaign. I called him the first war chief in office for over 100 years. This was in 1979 when Native Village started after the Okalee village closed. They put a Creek Indian in as manager. I couldn't work with him, so I quit. I told James I was going back to snake hunting.

"My wife threatened me with divorce if I didn't get out of the animal business. I was trained as a journeyman. So I did that for awhile," Skeets said. Denise soon realized Skeets was miserable if he wasn't working with animals.

Later, Skeets got a phone call from James. "Can you run Native Village for me? I got bit by a water moccasin and I'm in the hospital," said the chief.

"That was how I met my wife," said Skeets. "Back then, Denise was a nurse and I was in the hospital before James' accident with my leg swelled up twice its normal size."

"He was dating another nurse," said Denise. Denise kept going into her bedroom and coming up with photographs to document these stories.

"When you're hunting snakes, you should never put your hand down the hole. James was hunting harmless indigos and stuck his hand down a gopher hole. He got bit but didn't realize it, and put his hand down the hole again. It was a poisonous water moccasin. The bites on his hand swelled his whole arm up. The venom is close to the surface. It localizes and swells up. All blood circulation is cut off.

"There is a sixty percent chance of amputation. If you apply a tourniquet, there is a ninety percent chance of amputation. The snake's venom partially digests the food that they eat. People have seen blood oozing through the pores of the skin," said Skeets.

In James' second term he got more involved in politics. Nobody came close to him in any of his races. Nobody was a threat to him. He shared his ideas on bingo with other tribes. His popularity grew along with his influence.

Every year the Seminole Tribe holds a fair at the tribal headquarters that lasts for four days. At the fair, which is held every year in February, the tribal members make fry bread and all kinds of delicious food. Arts and crafts from many Indian tribes are on display.

Last year they held their first powwow in January.

"It was very successful. It was the best in the country," said Skeets proudly. "There is also a charity event called the 'Magical Village' where everything is decorated with Christmas lights."

Ross was in the movie *Live and Let Die* with James

Bond. He was the one who ran across the crocodiles' backs. He ended up with 180 stitches because he didn't make it the first time.

Ross owned two black leopards. The male was named Satan. One time he charged Skeets, so Ross warned everybody about him. The rule was that no one went into the leopard cage unless he had a backup. Two groups of tourists were coming in and they were shorthanded that day.

James was up in the office. "I heard shots and closed the gate to keep the people out. I ran back to the leopard cage and saw that Ross was badly wounded. He was covered with blood. Satan had attacked Ross and was biting him in the head.

"A girl we were training in animal husbandry had shot Satan and he was wounded. I dropped him. The animal had turned on Ross again.

"Ross never recovered from that. The female leopard had killed his dog, so she had to be put away too. All of Ross's nerve was gone. We went out and caught a nine and a half foot alligator. He shook and was frightened. He had nightmares where he saw Satan glaring at him.

"His buddy, Ross, and I were walking along a road in the mangroves. His friend played a trick on him by coming up from behind. Ross just crumbled into the fetal position. He died three months after Satan had attacked him," said Skeets.

James and Ross and Skeets were down in Jamaica hunting a man-eating crocodile named Bungus that had killed seven people. They were there with harpoons aimed and ready, when he popped up out of the ocean but they couldn't come near him. He looked like a dinosaur in the ocean. That crocodile hit the beach, then blasted through the seagrape trees into the river. The men beached the boat and went into the lake, but that was the only time they saw him in three years. They baited a trap for him with goats, but he always managed to steal the bait without getting caught.

James is an avid skin diver and bow hunter. When James and Skeets went hunting, he'd let Skeets catch the snakes. The night before Skeets got bit, he said, "You have to advertise. Well, we need you to get bit or something." He had a cigar in his mouth and was smoking it pensively.

"The next day, my arm was broken in nine places. I was in every tabloid all over the world. That alligator ended my skin diving. I used to do my own physical therapy. I'd pull my arm up until I couldn't stand the pain anymore. I knew I had to regain strength in the muscles. I was out of work for two and a half years as a result of it. My wife went back to college while I stayed home to raise the kids. That was the only good that came out of it. I gradually started drinking. James said to me, 'If you want your job, get help.' I just finished a five-week rehab program last week."

James and Skeets took a canoe trip along the old trading route where Ted Smallwood had a trading post in the 1800's down at Chokoloskee. There are thousands of miles of estuaries. Out on the flats they had to be really careful. At low tide, the oyster beds are out of the water, and then it rises to 2 or 3 feet of water at high tide. Their canoe was launched at the mouth of the river. The drainage canal got ploughed in because the government is trying to get it back the way it used to be. Dr. John the

Indian medicine man lived there. They left their cars behind and called ahead to arrange for other cars to pick them up.

"You'd swear you were in the Amazon," said Skeets. There were air plants and vanella orchids. The only other place they're found is at the pond apple preserve. James was the leader of this expedition. He brought along three bottles of Boone's Farm strawberry wine. Before they got to the river, a nine-foot alligator ran towards them up on the grass. James caught that gator by jumping it. What amazed them was the size of that gator and the conditions. They were in the swamp with all kinds of water reeds.

"James rode that gator right back into the saltwater. There was a journalist with us from the *Miami Herald* who did a story on it for the Sunday paper. We showed him where the army had marched," related Skeets.

He does a lot of guiding down there. It's all unexplored, uncharted territory. Perez was in this area. This was the old trading route where the Seminoles brought furs and feathers to sell. They came poling across the bay in their dugout canoes. They do a reenactment with traditional canoes. This place has huge blue crabs. There is a slight orange tint to the water because it contains botanic acid.

"Anyway, James was a little flirty on the Boone's Farm and couldn't turn around. The journalist was having a fine time, too. We were watching James as he pushed too hard. His canoe made a spiral and flipped over. He was cussin', but we laughed at him. The journalist wrote a real nice article about the adventure for the *Miami Herald*," said Skeets.

Skeets was seven years old when he caught his first alligator. The snakes out in the Everglades used to be really thick. When you hit route 27 you could slip your car on hundreds of snakes. You don't see those big snake migrations today. James and Skeets used to see 30 manatees in a herd. Indian boys enjoyed catching animals and reptiles. Skeets made his living all through school selling snakes and gators. He's been bitten nine times. Bill Haus, the owner of Miami Serpentarium, a tourist attraction, saved his life because he's allergic to anti-venom serum. Bill donated blood when Skeets needed it. Bill's been bitten 126 times, so his blood has anti-toxins in it, a neurotoxin from hemotoxin.

"What's always impressed me about James is his ability to use his ingenuity. Once we were riding around in a '54 Ford and we got stuck. There was one big branch sticking out overhead. James like to do things in the most primitive way. He enjoys using basic principles like leverage," observed Skeets.

"It might work," said James. "Let's throw a winch over that branch and hoist the engine out We can winch it up and then turn it around."

Back then Native Village was in full swing. James entertained there. They had plenty of lights and tiki torches. He did alligator wrestling for the crowds. James wrote a pageant which they put on for three years. At the old village there was a replica of Ft. Lauderdale with the army barracks and everything. The pageant was similar to a reenactment because it showed the dragoon forces. Chief Osceola was in it. They used old pictures going back to when the Spaniards first settled here up to where the Seminole is today.

James said in his pageant, "The white man came and these men were always hungry people."

"One time we were taking out a deer to James' grandfather's hunting camp. Deer are very important in the Seminole culture. The gift of a deer shows great honor and respect." James' grandfather was there sitting on a stump. His camp was on a long road way out in the wilderness.

At Native Village there was a chimpanzee named Jim and a pig named Billie. Ross would call them and James would look around, thinking he was being called. One time they had some crocodiles that were being shipped. They put them in a truck freezing compartment to keep them quiet and turned the thermometer down to 40 degrees.

When James came back, the crocodiles were frozen solid. Someone had turned the thermometer down to zero. James figured the culprit wasn't far away. It turned out to be Jim, the chimpanzee, who was watching when they unlatched the door. He imitated them, opened the freezer and turned down the thermometer that governed the temperature.

James always said he would form his own family. There are the dynasties in all cultures.

"I've always had this feeling that James was a king and I was his knight ready to serve him," said Skeets.

Chief Billie is a very determined man. When they were building one of the chickees, James said, "I have to do it my way because the architect couldn't figure it out."

When James was working on a biological study at Big Cypress, he adopted a pet anhinga bird that he had found. He fed it and raised it, watching its feathers change to black as it matured. The tame anhinga would come when James called it. One day he came home from work and the bird was gone.

James has a friend named Mitchell Cypress, one of the councilmen for the Seminole tribe, who went to Clewiston High School with James. They had fought back-to-back against the white boys, who didn't like the Indians.

Mitchell came up to James and told him about their wonderful meal. An anhinga had come up to Mitchell because the bird had been used to getting a fish from James. The anhinga was very tame. It ran up to Mitchell, expecting a fish. Mitchell clubbed the bird, and brought it home to his large family of nine for dinner.

"We just had an anhinga and it was delicious!" exclaimed Mitchell in church the next Sunday. James was devastated. They had cooked James' pet. James just glared at Mitchell. To get Mitchell back, James was working construction building chickees. He came across a rattlesnake that he needed for display at Native Village. He stored the snake in his toolbox. Mitchell, who was working with him, bent over and looked at the ground.

"What happened, Mitchell?" asked James. Mitchell had lost the screw to hold on his glasses.

"You can get a screwdriver in my toolbox," answered James roguishly.

As Mitchell started putting his hand in, James shouted "Don't put your hand in there, you fool. I have a snake in there!"

Chapter 8

Chief Billie—The Hunter

The den was well-hidden in the thick vegetation of the swamp. This sinewy golden panther had stalked deer since she was a cub. Her mother had trained her to hunt and she had followed her mother's example. This night she could find nothing in her normal terrain.

The panther roamed further away from her den. She prowled at night when it was cool. Her quest took her miles away from her familiar territory. Game was scarce this time of year.

Suddenly she heard something. Was it a raccoon, a rabbit or a deer? She stopped abruptly. She sniffed the air. Her long tail flicked swiftly. The large cat crouched down on the grass with her front legs poised and her back legs tensed ready to spring. She moved ahead slowly.

A light came out of nowhere. She blinked her yellow-green eyes. Three men appeared from behind a palmetto tree. Chief Billie, Robb Tiller and an Indian boy were out hunting for alligators to stock their wildlife farm. They came up on the panther who had lifted her head and was ready to pounce. James grabbed his gun and aimed. The two others ran back to the jeep and hid inside afraid.

She dropped down dead, prey to the nocturnal hunters she didn't know existed in her world. Florida panthers are becoming more and more scarce. Like the Indians, their hunting grounds are being eroded by citrus and sugarcane. The chief was very careful skinning the panther because he wanted the pelt to be perfectly preserved. Killing the panther was part of his religious training to attain a deeper knowledge of shaman ways.

Robb Tiller wanted to make himself invisible when the policemen arrived. He was sweeping the dirt floor of the chickee where the panther was being cured, and the police didn't even interrogate him, thanks to his training in the State Department.

The arrest didn't take place then, however, because the chief made it very clear he wasn't going to jail. There must have been a question in the police officer's minds, because they didn't bring him in. It was a matter of white justice versus Indian justice. James Billie tested the law. The case attracted national attention. It was one of the biggest issues since Justice Marshall's Supreme Court decision to make Indian reservations sovereign nations. The outcome determined the jurisdiction of the head of a sovereign nation, Chief James Billie of the Seminoles.

Luckily, the trial was held in Hendry County, where James Billie grew up. The main controversy stemmed around the state prosecutor, Assistant State Attorney Robert Greene, who believed the state had legitimate jurisdiction in the case, but admitted that it was a very complex issue. There were many people on the jury who had known James Billie as a young man, but denied it so they could be involved. Coverage of the trial was state-wide.

"I remember interviewing Chief Billie during the trial. He's very smart," said Chuck Eldred who was working as a radio reporter at the time for a Florida station covering the story. Chuck is now head of the film liaison office for Palm Beach County in West Palm Beach.

According to the *Miami Herald's* story of December 13, 1983, federal agents charged Fred Smith, Seminole Tribal President, with the crime of illegally selling feathers of federally protected bald eagles and other protected birds. He pled guilty and received a $25,000 fine.

But this panther case differed on several points. The Chief had not intended to sell the hide of the panther. He was carrying out an ancient religious ritual to become a shaman. It was a jurisdictional principle in the minds of the prosecution. Furthermore, the panther shooting carried on a teaching tradition of the Native American culture. It took place on the Indian reservation, which is Seminole soil.

At that time, the number of surviving panthers throughout the Everglades was estimated at between 18 and 30. If found guilty of the crime, the Seminole chief could have been imprisoned for a maximum of five years. The fine might have been as much as $5,000.

The case brought Chief Billie notoriety as a big animal killer. The panther is considered an endangered species by both state and federal agencies. The skull and hide of the panther was found by Florida Game and Fresh Water Fish Commission Investigators on December 2, 1983.

The national interest in this case spread phenomenally. *Time Magazine,* the *New York Times* and *CBS Nightly News* all covered the story. Indian justice versus white justice was, once again, in conflict.

The outcome of the case was, in part, a tribute to Chief Billie's character. He was tried by a jury who knew his reputation as a fighter in Vietnam. He had won court battles for his tribe against Sheriffs Ed Stack and Robert Butter-worth to obtain smoke shops and bingo parlors.

The jury was sympathetic for several reasons. Chief Billie was a Seminole. The people of Glades and Hendry counties were respectful of Native American ways. Most of them were farmers and cattlemen. All of them hunted or fished. They did not view these natural sports as criminal behavior, but as normal pastimes.

On the flip side, he had killed a male panther that may have helped bring the panther population back from near extinction. Panthers live 35 or 40 years in captivity but only 5 to 10 years in the wild. He disobeyed a law for the benefit of the small remaining wild panther population that is struggling to survive naturally in a terrain invaded by air boats, hunters and a diminishing supply of food.

In Osceola's day, hunting was one of the Indian's only way of earning money for rifles that they purchased from Spanish traders from Cuba. The value of a deerskin was only twenty-five cents per pound. Good otter skins were enormously in demand. They were each worth three dollars. Raccoon skins brought twelve and a half cents each. Wildcat or panther skins brought only twenty-five cents each.

It is sad to think of the dwindling number of beautiful wild cats crouched languidly in the trees of the swamp. They have been part of Florida's ecosystem for millions of years and the fact that they are on the verge of extinction because of overhunting means that enough effort has not been made to assure that their lineage will continue.

The Seminole shaman Sonnie Billie said, "There is very powerful medicine in the panther. I will say that I am very proud of James for shooting the panther." He described James Billie as a bundle carrier for the Green Corn Dance, an ancient secret ritual held each spring in the Everglades.

The aftermath of the panther trial hampered James' musical career. He was acquitted of the charge, but had to pay in other ways.

"They accused me of killing every animal that ever lived. There were pickets in front of the places I performed," commented James.

Controversial, James is not afraid of anything. He believes it is a great weakness to show fear. He is proud of all that he has accomplished. He continues to push on in every sphere.

The clash between white laws and Indian laws culminated in this trial. It is a tribute to the chief that he stands up for what he believes. Dr. Charles Fairbanks, retired University of Florida professor, attested "The fact that the head was cut off is significant. I am pretty sure ritual was involved in some way."

Chief Billie and the panther.

Chapter 9

Important Role Model

S eminoles have never been like white men. They are quiet; they have expert reflexes. They are strong, observant, and eagle-eyed. These are the qualities a Seminole needs to survive in the Everglades. Seminole leaders have these qualities in abundance.

Seminoles traditionally relied on wild game for food. Therefore, they ate everything they killed, much as the plains Indians were dependent on the buffalo for their subsistence. Chief Jim Billie's freezer is full of deer meat, soft shell turtle, alligator and the other animals he has hunted.

Not concerned with public opinion, the Seminole chief is very protective of his tribe. In an article in *The Sun Tattler* on May 19, 1984 he stated, "Members of the tribe, especially the younger ones, for far too long have had a defeatist attitude. They've been knocked down so often that many don't want to get up. They don't even want to try."

Out at the reservation, one of his 15-year old boys was beaten up by a white man who was trying to make him drink beer. The chief is very concerned with being a good role model to these teenagers. He wanted to know who was responsible for treating his boy in a bullying manner. This abuse will not be tolerated, for Chief Billie has a strong manner and strong sense of justice for his people.

James, with fury in his eyes, wishes that the bullies had stayed around to take their punishment. The first building he erected on Big Cypress was a gymnasium so that the Indians could stay physically fit.

There is also a large rodeo grounds where the tribe sponsors native Aztec firedancers from Mexico City, country and blue grass musicians, comedians, rodeo contests, fireworks and all kinds of entertainment.

"I want to get away from defeatist thinking," the chief says. "I want to build confidence among the tribe. Let the people get used to the idea that they are somebody, that they have culture, that they can achieve.

"I want to make sure they get the opportunity to do what they want. . .and not what somebody else wants."

"The chief's very goal-oriented," stated Dave Vopnford, president of **Tomorrow's Stars,** who recorded his music tapes. "If he says something, he means it. People listen to him."

An old Indian prophecy foresaw that one day all the Seminole customs and stories would be lost. Chief James Billie is determined not to let this happen, for that would be the end of the Seminoles' world.

What will prevent losing the old ways is keeping the interest in them alive. Courage to buck the system has helped Jim Billie, since he was elected chief in 1979, gain power for his tribe. His style is very aggressive. "Go for the throat, cut their heads off, ask questions later," like a war chief. Five Florida reservations—Hollywood, Big Cypress, Brighton, Tampa and Immokalee—are under his tutelage.

When James Billie came back from Vietnam, he tried

to get elected chief of his tribe. But the Seminoles were suspicious of this upstart half-breed. In order to gain their trust, he decided to train the young people in self-determination. There were several avenues he chose. One was through the sale of Indian crafts, which was familiar to them. Seminoles had been earning their living in this manner since trading with the Spanish. Other ways were new. He hired the young men to work on a chickee construction crew. In this enterprise, they became more self-sufficient. His popularity grew among his people. Only after he had proved himself, did James Billie get elected to the prestigious position of chief.

His unorthodox ways are controversial. He is not afraid to challenge the system, especially if he can change it for his tribe's benefit. The results have been staggering. He has gained the respect not only of the Seminoles, but of the entire Native American community.

He has added many items to his medicine pouch. The claw of a panther when it reaches up to catch a bird is there. The tip of a panther's tail when it flicks its tail back and forth waiting for the kill is there.

The panther killing set off a wave of controversy. The Florida Game and Freshwater Fish Commission accused Billie of killing the endangered animal illegally. He was charged on a felony count of killing a panther and a misdemeanor count of possessing the animal's remains. The panther was found decapitated with its skull and hide hung on two poles outside Billie's thatched hut on the Big Cypress Seminole Indian reservation.

Chief Billie is an inspiring leader. His aim, when he returned from Vietnam was "to make money." He had absorbed the lessons he learned in the military when he went on reconnaissance missions in planes and helicopters over the landscape. "Always have an evasion plan," he learned.

The chief is like a thoroughbred—speedy, highstrung and competitive. His thoughts are like quicksilver, tumbling out in the form of stories. He can go in 50 directions at once. He systematically solves problems everyday. He asks questions all the time. "Let me alone," he commanded, as he was telling a story and didn't want to be interrupted.

He claims that Disney stole the folk tales of the Seminoles and animated them for children. The mission of reclaiming what rightly belongs to the Native Americans occupies his thoughts and sets his direction.

Chief Billie's curiosity is boundless. He and his friend Sammy Nelson were going to get jobs wrestling alligators for the circus. They hurried down to U.S. 1 in Hollywood where Circus City had pitched their colorful tents. There was a long row of cages where the circus lions were kept. Unable to resist the temptation to examine the lions, James bolted away from Sammy and found a cage where the bars didn't completely close. He stared at the massive paws of the cat, who had his eyes half-closed.

"I couldn't believe that a man could go into a cage with 8 or 10 lions that had their claws. We had a lion that had been declawed at the Indian Village."

Gingerly, he felt the lion's huge paw. He examined the veins or tendons bulging out from the fur. He looked at the lion inquisitively. The lion looked back under half-closed lids, still not moving. There was about six inches under the cage where the bars didn't reach. The lion's paws were crossed casually, protruding out from under the bars. James couldn't bear it. He took his hand and

96

pulled on the lion's mane to make the lion show his paw. Instinct triggered the lion's quick reaction. His lightning quick claws flexed and dug into James' right arm, pulling out the tendon. James was locked in a vice-like grip and couldn't get away. He screamed for his friend Sammy who tried to free him, but the lion wouldn't let go. He grabbed James' leg with his other paw and "Almost gave me another asshole," in James' words.

The lion had such a strong grip that Sammy had to run for a hammer to bang on its paw so the lion would let go. He finally got his friend's arm extricated from the clutches of the deadly attack. The lion had embedded his claw in James arm and was holding him captive. The claws do not retract easily once they are clenched. Imagine the surprise and astonishment that James had caused everyone involved! When they took him to the hospital, one of the nurses exclaimed, "It looks like a lion got you!"

Everyone laughed, never realizing that indeed it had. Chief James Billie had proven beyond a shadow of a doubt that the lions in the ring at Circus City had not been declawed. This discovery left him permanent scars. Another time James pointed to his appendix scar and said with a sad face, "White man cut me." Only after getting the desired sympathy, did the wily chief admit it was from an operation.

Phil Genovar, Robb Tiller and the chief went to Washington to urge the formation of an Indian reservation in St. Augustine. Phil had on a wide, handpainted tie. There they met Bill Hart, Senior news advisor for President Ronald Reagan. Reagan's staff read every newspaper all over the world and then compiled a news summary for him which Bill Hart gave to the President each morning.

While they were in the White House, Robb Tiller found President Reagan's office and sat at his desk.

Joel Frank (far left), James (center) and Skeets (far right) on a fall hunting trip.

On a hunting trip in Idaho in 1990, Skeets told of the time he and James were retracing the trail that Lewis and Clark took on their way west. Chief Joseph had passed through this territory on his way to Canada. James made a bet as to who would get to Moose Creek first. Skeets never made it there and neither did the chief because the trail was too overgrown. There is a photo of the men on the trip with James clowning around by holding a cup under his horse's tail.

Park manager and sales manager for Thousand Adventures campground and marina, Roger Alten came from the Great Lakes region of the United States in 1965

James lands his plane on the levee.

down to Moore Haven, Florida. Dave Vopnford bought the only campground situated on Army Corp of Engineers land inside the levee on Lake Okeechobee. Roger came with the package. A tall affable man, Roger once went down to the Keys and "In about a week I became a conch." He remembers the time Chief Billie landed his airplane on the levee. "He sings with our **Tomorrow's Stars** singers like Don Frost and Vicki Lee. We have a recreation hall over at Sportsman's Village, our RV park on the other side of the locks. During the season, we hold

99

shows there. I sell memberships to Thousand Adventures."

"He sings like Johnny Cash," observed Roger. "I'm impressed with what he's done for his people who were chased into the Everglades. He's done quite a bit for them. Seminoles may never again live like they used to. Our members go down there to Big Cypress reservation."

At the reception desk for Billie Swamp Safari at Big Cypress, Georgia Turner remembers the first time she met Chief Billie.

"My husband Ard introduced him to me. 'This is my Indian brother,' he said. James is teaching Ard to fly as a surprise to his father, Pete Turner, an army pilot.

"How many beads and blankets do you want for her?" asked James.

"I've worked for the tribe for three years at the school. I used to be a substitute teacher, a bookkeeper, the school nurse, and I repaired copy machines. Nobody else seemed to want to do it." Georgia is a jovial woman with a warm smile and a twinkle in her eye.

"Now James says to me, 'I can hardly get my arms around you.' He's got a good sense of humor." There is a bunch of T-shirts in a box ready to put on hangers. James' picture is on the front flying an airplane and smoking a cigar.

"Next weekend, we're having a big arts and crafts fair here. We're expecting to get in a shipment any day now. Where should I put all these?" Georgia starts hanging up the T-shirts on racks.

Skeets appears. His wife, Denise, is going down to Miami to do her first animal show. It will cost $350 to rent a panther just for one night. In Florida it is illegal to turn any non-native animal loose. For example, the brown lizard that is everywhere originally came here from Haiti. Palm Beach is the summer home of red-headed parrots that spend their winters in Mexico and summers in palm trees around the Breakers Hotel.

One of the guides reports a 180-lb. panther was spotted out in the hog hunting area. Perhaps it is the one that killed the male antelope that used to roam around the Safari pastures. Panthers prowl around the Everglades, looking for birds and small animals to catch.

When a wild hog is shot the guides skin and quarter it. The meat is redder than the domestic port that you buy. It should be cured because it has fat on it. The meat makes fine sausages. It resembles the wild pig found in Hawaii. The meat can be kept for five or six days.

"I wonder what it costs to get the head stuffed?" said my husband Thom, as we drove home and he contemplated going on a wild boar hunt with the Seminole guides.

Skeets told us about some Indians who refuse to believe in either the Miccosukees, led by Billy Cypress who was elected tribal chairman in 1987, or the Seminoles. They are called the Independent Indians. These Indians still stay in their chickees in the old manner and live on state land. There are approximately 5,000 Indians living at the present time in Florida.

The mayor of Miami, Marco LaFalco, was attending a formal dinner party for Don Johnson to celebrate the hit TV series *Miami Vice.* Chief Billie and Robb Tiller drove to the party in "Blackie," a special 6.9 edition car made for ambassadors by Mercedes Benz with a custom chrome bumper, a rear door longer than the standard model, an ambassadorial back headrest, an adjustment that raised and lowered the chassis and a high-speed engine.

High society was in attendance. At the party, Kirk Douglas Jr. was mingling with many other Miami celebrities. Chief James Billie was wearing his traditional Seminole jacket and skirt for the occasion. As the crowd gasped, James suddenly shot out from the wings like a cannon with an alligator named Long Jaws behind him. He pulled the 12-foot alligator on a portable dolly, much to the disbelief of the crowd and terror of one guest who had formerly poo-pooed the announcement of an alligator's presence with the acknowledgement: "Oh, I have one in my garden pool." Her jaw dropped when she got one good look at the size of Long Jaws!

The alligator snapped his jaws, practically taking off one guest's hand. James delighted in the dinner guests' reaction to his Native American cultural exhibition.

James strives to set a good example in his role as chief. The trait of physical courage is one that James exhibits in all his endeavors. As a shelter for his rodeo exhibition, he once built a log cabin in one day.

He likes people who show initiative and tries to instill this characteristic in his tribal members. Competitive in everything, James is aware that the Native Americans will need to help one another learn the white man's games. He encourages excellence in many ways.

James loves to fly. Courses on helicopter and fixed wing flying are available free to Seminoles at a ground school James established on Big Cypress reservation. He does not spare any expense to make sure the Seminole Tribe has the technology and know-how to compete in today's modern world.

Chapter 10

The Fight for Bingo

Chief James Billie, since taking office, has raised the tribal annual income from $500,000 to over $57 million. Sixty percent of this money comes from gaming. Economic times were hard for the Seminole tribe when James Billie was elected chief in 1979, so the main driving force behind his actions was to win independence for his tribe. When he realized his chickee construction business was forcing Seminoles to be dependent on the white man, he tried other tactics. He explored other opportunities.

"I looked at the white man's weaknesses," said James. "Casinos were controlled by organized crime at that time. Jai Alai was controlled by a Latin American group. Dog tracks were run by someone else. So I thought of bingo."

He took his idea to the Archbishop of Miami, Archbishop Maloney, and asked for his blessing. The chief not only received his blessing, but a compliment from the leader of the Catholic church that bingo was a good money-making scheme for the Seminoles.

James and the Archbishop proved to be right. The first building that the Seminoles erected, the Hollywood Bingo Hall, was constructed in 1979. This moneymaking facility opened its doors in December. The hall is managed by George Simon and "Butch" Weisman. Some sources say that Meyer Lansky—the financial genius behind La Cosa Nostra—may have provided the initial financing for the Hollywood operation through a legitimate bank loan. This speculation can never be validated because Meyer Lansky died in 1983 at age 80 in Miami Beach. In the film *The Godfather Part II,* the character of Hyman Roth was based on Mr. Lansky.

The Archdiocese of Miami went one step further by providing a grant of $33,000, most of which went to help pay Attorney Steve H. Whilden's salary. Hired in 1977, Whilden proved to be a linchpin in the bingo phenomenon. He knew how to obtain confidential information due to his training in the U.S. State Department. He had also worked in the Office of Management and Budget, serving as a White House liaison. His two diplomatic tours in Vietnam made him a perfect deal maker for the Seminole tribe.

"He was good at getting information on people and I also had access to all that information," said Chief Billie.

Steve Whilden expanded the Indian's land holdings, negotiated contracts and fought off the IRS's attempt to tax tribal income, but along the way he made enemies. For five years, he and James pushed the Seminole Tribe of Florida into the economic battlefield like the militant leaders they were.

Chief Billie told the story that was to be Steve Whilden's final blunder. Attorney Jim Shore, a blind Seminole, had been hired by the tribe in 1980.

"Jim Shore's wife came into his office. Both he and Steve were working for the tribe at time. Jim's office was smaller than Steve's. Jim's wife didn't like that. She complained about it being too dark. Steve replied by asking what difference it made since Jim couldn't see anyway.

Word of that story got around the tribe. Marcellus Osceola fired him," said James.

"Whilden was a snake," Marcellus Osceola is quoted as saying to the *Miami Herald* in 1983. "I fired Steve because I wanted an Indian to run the reservation. He served his purpose."

Whilden also aroused suspicions with his choice of business associates. A Miami newspaper reported that two men involved in his deals on Indian reservations in Massachusetts, Minnesota, and Washington were convicted felons with records for multiple counts of fraud and forgery. Whilden said at the time that he had no knowledge of their criminal pasts. He is now working at a small U.S. Army base in Germany as a civilian lawyer for the military.

"I am the head of a sovereign nation," Billie points out. "We may be small, but we are the equivalent of any third world nation in the world."

Take a ride down route 441 in Hollywood. There are several smoke shops, some open 24 hours a day, where the Seminoles sell their cigarettes. Manufactured trailers full of cartons and cartons of cigarettes provide drive-through windows where cars and trucks line up all day and night to buy their tobacco at discount prices.

Travel a bit further. On the right is the Hollywood Bingo Hall. Bright lights advertise the daily jackpots to passing cars. Airplanes with banners flying draw men and women in from West Palm Beach to Miami to play in hopes of winning the big pot.

Why is Indian bingo so popular? One reason is the amount of the prize money. No church or fund-raising group can consistently offer $50,000 in prizes. Like other forms of gaming, bingo players want the chance and thrill of winning big. Although years ago the rules for declaring bingo winnings were looser—participants would take out their cash in paper bags—today the IRS keeps close tabs on where the money goes.

Florida's policy towards casinos is that they are illegal. However, there are loopholes. "The federal statute says that if the state's policy is to allow certain types of gaming, it could be that the tribe can do other forms of gaming," explains Joel Frank, head of the Seminole Gaming Commission in Washington.

"Until 1993, the Bureau of Indian Affairs lent money to the tribes for bingo hall construction. This year a congressman from Wisconsin complained, saying it was morally not right to encourage the tribes to get into gambling. A lot of politicians and commercial gaming businessmen would like to end Indian gaming. As of January, 1993 the B.I.A. no longer lends money for this purpose," Frank said.

"If the state doesn't prohibit it, then it's negotiable," added Frank. "This issue has been our lawyers' bread and butter for the last several years. The only involvement on the part of the Indian Gaming Regulatory Act is to approve the ordinances and to approve management. This responsibility rests with the Secretary of the Interior, trustee for the Indian tribes. Bruce Babbitt's our "great white father."

"Back when Andrew Jackson was president, Chief Justice Marshall fought a test of wills with him by declaring the Supreme Court doctrine that Indian tribes were a nation within a nation. The issue was could the Supreme Court order a President? The tribes have always maintained that they had sovereignty.

"The state is saying that it is immune from law suits

and it cannot be sued by foreign governments," explained Frank. "The state collects a tax from those casinos on cruise ships."

"Even if casino gambling is illegal in the eyes of the state, it may be legal at the county level. The attorney general says it's illegal. However, it's up to the sheriff and county prosecutor whether they want to enforce it. Then it's not a state issue anymore."

"In 1974, the Florida State legislature in an attempt to get out of law enforcement, founded 'special improvement districts.' This was so that they didn't have to pay for law enforcement. These districts were put under their own jurisdiction, similar to a county. This made the Seminole reservations a county in their own right. The Miccosukees are also a county themselves," stated Frank.

"In the 1920's Florida was riddled with casinos. Then it was the county sheriffs who cleaned that up. Then in the 50's, the Johnson Act prohibited the transporting of gambling devices across state lines."

Osley Saunooke remembers meeting Chief James Billie in 1972 when he was running the Indian Village in Hollywood.

"He's always been a promoter," said Saunooke. "He's got boundless energy."

Attorney Saunooke was the first director of the United Southeastern Tribes headquartered in Sarasota. He headed the business development committee for the Florida Governor's Council on Indian Affairs in 1973 and 1974 under Ruben Askew.

"When we started the smoke shops (a store that sells discount cigarettes), it gave the Seminoles flexible money. Before this business took off, the government meted out money, but it told them how to spend it. They needed flexible dollars for economic development." Attorney Saunooke is a member of the Cherokee tribe.

Marcellus Osceola opened the first smoke shop in 1977. James promised Marcellus he wouldn't go into it. That was when Howard Tommie was chairman of the tribe. Joe Dan was also interested in starting a smoke shop.

The sheriff of Broward County, Ed Stack, took the tribe to court to contest this venture. Later, Robert Butterworth, Ed Stack's successor as Broward County Sheriff, went after the Seminole Tribe's bingo operations.

"Both of them did us a favor," stated Saunooke. These operations went on to become lucrative sources of revenue for the Seminole Tribe of Florida.

The Clinton administration has appointed Ada Deer assistant secretary of the Department of the Interior. She is a Menominee Indian from Wisconsin who ran for congress but was unsuccessful. Her tribe outside of Green Bay was one of the ones that was terminated in 1958. Within days of the tribe's termination, the tribal land became government land and was sold on the public market. Now the Menominees have achieved federal recognition. Ada Deer almost singlehandedly got her tribe restored and took over ownership of what little land the tribe still has.

There are two categories of membership for Indian tribes today. The Shinnecock Indians on eastern Long Island are a state recognized tribe. New York State has designated them a tribe, but the federal government has not. Florida's Seminoles are federally recognized.

The United States government has no trust responsibility for non-federally recognized tribes. Federal recognition elevates a tribe to a different status. The Department of the Interior recognizes 515 Indian tribes. Federal recognition is often a long process requiring about eight years of documentation. All of these Native American tribes have negotiated treaties or have established a trust relationship with the United States government.

Bingo has certainly helped some tribes enter the business arena in a big way. Whether this will remain the mainstay of tribal income remains to be seen. For now, the controversy continues.

"The Seminole tribe has always maintained that it is a sovereign government," states Joel Frank. "When the issue of bingo came up, the states maintained that they had jurisdiction. However, since the courts have modified the intent of Congress only where criminal jurisdiction applies, the tribe had complete jurisdiction because the issue was regulatory and not criminal. In Florida, if certain forms of gaming are permitted, tribes can negotiate those types of gaming in their compacts with the state."

Roy Diamond, director of Billie Swamp Safari, has been involved with the tribe since March of 1985. He came on board with a group called Bingo Entertainment at a time when the tribe already had bingo at the Tampa and Hollywood reservations.

"Chief Billie hired me to be the general manager of a bingo hall out in Auburn, Washington, for the Muckleshoot Indians. He was supposed to be there for six months, but was there only a few days," Roy said.

Roy was transferred to Red Rock, Oklahoma. (pop. 376) The Seminoles formed a joint venture with the Otoe-Missouria Indian tribe to run bingo there.

There were problems in Oklahoma because so many Indians had been relocated there by the "Trail of Tears" removal campaign in the 1830's. This forced removal by the federal government created enormous hardship for the Indians. Over 4,000 men, women and children died during this arduous march. With so many tribes and such sparse population, bingo was risky business. If all the Oklahoma tribes were to go into bingo, there would not be enough profit to keep the hall in business. Sure enough, in September of '86 the hall closed.

Roy Diamond comments, "With Chief Billie, you never know what's going to happen next. We might go off to Clewiston and be gone for three days. He is a man who beats his own drum. He has missed dinner appointments with President Carter because he does what he wants when he wants. He could care less who he leaves sitting behind."

After his Oklahoma stint, Roy wound up in Watertown, South Dakota at the bingo hall of the Sioux tribe. In January, 1987, he was hired to run the Big Cypress Hall, but didn't get along with the general manager. A month later, the Big Cypress Hall closed because they weren't making any money. In February, 1988, another group came in, but they were also unable to make a go of it.

Investment Resources, owned by Stan Talby, hired Roy in April, 1989. The Big Cypress bingo hall was opened again. Whether the distance to get to it was too great, or whether the expectations were too high, in July, 1989 the hall closed again.

In September, 1989, the Seminoles and Bob Tate in North Carolina were planning to form a joint venture wherein Bonus Bingo with a million dollar pot would be run once a month. All the plans were in place for this megaventure. Roy Diamond went up to learn Bob Tate's game. Then hurricane Hugo hit and the Bonus Bingo plans were shattered. Roy stayed in North Carolina for the following six months, working for Bob Tate.

In December, 1990, Roy became the tribal bingo representative for the Miccosukee Indians at their hall on Tamiami Trail. This lasted until December of 1992 when Roy was hired by Billie Swamp Safari to direct the construction for the Seminole Tribe of Florida.

Roy's ex-wife Pat is Chief Billie's secretary. "She can read him better than he can read himself," Roy observed. "James has different moods for different people. I don't flock after him to let him know what I've done. I see what mood he's in before I give him my report.

"Yesterday, he was with some people and he seemed to be in a jovial mood. Then another group came up and he was in a mixed mood. So I saved what I was going to say to him.

"He says what he wants and does what he wants. He rode on Air Force One with President Carter, Governor Graham and Senator Van Poole."

Roy Diamond is presently adding a tiki bar to the alligator pit arena. Future plans include a refreshment area and bar where acholic beverages will be served.

"We don't need a license, but we're going to get one because our tribal elders want us to do it that way," the director announced.

After all the white man has taken from Native Americans—his land, his animals, his horses, his women, why was permission to run bingo games such a hot issue that had to go all the way to the Supreme Court?

There are several possibilities. The fact that all churches and private clubs were allowed to use bingo as a fund-raising technique is not disputed. These organizations were part of the establishment. Bringing whites onto the reservations was perhaps the bigger issue.

The history of the Indians' conflicts with the white man goes back to the discovery of the New World by Europeans. With the arrival of Columbus by ship in 1492, there began a relentless destruction of the people along with their religious beliefs as well as their customary Native American way of life.

The Seminoles are a resilient tribe. They have existed in the swamps of the Everglades for many generations. They have defied attempts to relocate them in Arkansas, to change their ways, and to keep them down. Chief James Billie has led his tribe in clash after clash by challenging the white man's laws. His victories have been hard-fought because he is a Native American warrior.

In 1981, the Seminoles purchased eight and a half acres in Tampa near a Seminole burial ground. Tampa Assistant City Attorney Josephine Stafford said, "We thought they were just going to build a memorial, maybe sell some souvenirs...." Instead, they used the space for a six-window drive-in smoke shop and an enormous bingo hall.

"Sometimes the chief can be difficult," said Roy. "Especially with those who can't read his moods."

Why is the Big Cypress bingo hall full of surplus army equipment instead of bingo players in 1995? Perhaps the right person to run it has not been found. Perhaps that person will come along any day now. In the meantime, the chief is not sitting around contemplating it. He is thinking in terms of higher stakes.

"The governor had it sitting around on his desk and hadn't done anything with it, so I sued him," stated Chief

Billie about the deal between the Seminoles and the State of Florida for casino gambling.

If history repeats itself, the Seminole Tribe will soon be in the driver's seat with high stakes gambling similar to the Mashantucket Pequot's casino in Connecticut which, according to the *Seminole Tribune,* has hurt Donald Trump, who is suing the federal government because he contends that "the Indian Gaming Regulatory Act is unconstitutional and gives tribes an unfair advantage." The tribal leaders, with characteristic humor, "have dubbed the bills the 'Donald Trump Protection Act,' just as they nicknamed the bill that sought to raise the casino stakes from $5-10 bets to $100 at a proposed casino site in South Dakota the 'Costner Bill.'"

At a House Native American Affairs Subcommittee hearing, Rep. Bill Richardson from New Mexico, the chairman of the subcommittee, said that any changes from the 1988 law must consider the three "fundamental pillars" in place to protect tribes. These are 1) the regulation of Indian affairs is strictly a federal function, 2) states have always been excluded from federal-tribal relations, and 3) that tribes have sovereignty over their land.

Furthermore, the *Seminole Tribune* writes, "Indian gaming takes in about $6 billion a year and is about 3 percent of the national gambling industry. Since the Indian Gaming Regulatory Act was passed in 1988, about 260 gaming halls, including bingo halls, have opened on 170 reservations in 24 states."

Back in the 1800's, the Bureau of Indian Affairs was under the Department of Defense due to the nature of the relations between Native Americans and whites. Army posts were set up to keep Indians on their reservations.

113

Then, when the army was focused on national problems, a government restructuring in the 1930's placed the B.I.A. under the Department of the Interior.

"A lot of politicians and commercial business owners would like to see Indian gaming stopped," observed Joel Frank. "Until January, 1993, the economic development of bingo was encouraged by the B.I.A. Then a congressman from Wisconsin complained and said it is morally wrong to encourage tribes to get into gambling.

"The Environmental Protection Agency has jurisdiction on Indian reservations. Each region is different, but the states have no jurisdiction in this area."

Back in 1953, Congress attempted to get the states behind Indian issues in support of termination. Florida was one of eight states to go along with Congress. However, the courts have modified the intent of Congress.

Not all of Chief Billie's plans come to fruition in the way he expects. He was planning to take the bingo corporation public on the Denver, Colorado, penny stock exchange. This public offering would have raised 150 million dollars for the tribe to finance their bingo operations. However, on the eve of the public offering, two of the underwriters, Sidney Bernstein and Larry Monberg were killed in an airplane crash on their way to Denver. Their plane, a DC-10, was caught in a wind shear, and nearly everyone aboard was killed. When this method of sponsorship fell through, James got backing from a local bank.

James is flamboyant in his problem-solving approaches. It is to James' credit that his direct tactics get results. He is humble when appropriate, such as asking Congress for favorable legislation. No wonder he has accomplished so much!

Skeets, Robb, and Chief Billie went to Washington, D. C. With them was a large alligator that they introduced on the Senate floor. The sight of an actual alligator in the Senate must have emphasized the Indian's point. Chief James Billie always plays to win.

Casino gambling has been thrown into the federal arena. The Seminole Tribe of Florida sued the state for refusing to negotiate whether to allow casino gambling on tribal lands. The U.S. Circuit Court of Appeals in Atlanta ruled on January 18, 1994 that the Seminole tribe can't sue the state.

"But the tribe can bypass the courts and bring its complaint against the state directly to the U.S. Department of the Interior, which regulates Native American affairs, the court ruled," according to the *Miami Herald,* January 20, 1994.

The Secretary of the Interior, Bruce Babbitt, is favorably inclined to negotiate gaming for the Seminoles, as he did in Arizona. There, "Secretary Babbitt struck an agreement between the state and the tribes that allowed more than 5,000 electronic slot machines on tribal reservations in March, 1993."

"It's great for us," said Bruce Rogow, the Seminoles' attorney and a Nova Southeastern University law professor. "The state really shot itself in the foot."

"We lost, but we really won," was how Chief Billie summed up their courtroom victory. He has consistently used the law to battle for Native American economic progress. This latest example will bring millions of dollars into the already fat tribal coffers.

Chief Billie lands his Bell Jet Ranger.
Earnest Hillard shakes hands with Charles Kirkpatrick.

The referendum known on Florida's ballot as Amendment 8 proposed competition to the Seminoles. If passed, it would have brought a limited number of luxury resort casinos to the state, along with five riverboat casinos and casinos at greyhound tracks, thoroughbred tracks and Jai Alai frontons. In November, 1994, the amendment was defeated by a two-thirds majority of voters.

Chapter 11

Chief Billie: The Diplomat, the Benefactor, and the Cop to his People

*A*ttorney Jack Skelding has worked in Tallahassee for Howard Tommie and then for Chief James Billie when he was elected chairman of the tribe in 1979. He litigated the case for cigarettes and has worked with Billie ever since.

"James is a natural leader and decision maker. He's extremely good with people. I'm continually amazed at his powerful abilities. He's matured a lot over the years. I see a lot of political leaders. A lot of my friends have worked their way up. They need to be good politicians and good leaders. He's both. Many people don't realize that the Seminole tribe is a separate nation and government unto itself.

"The only time we disagree is if I'm too cautious. James doesn't want to show fear. He wants to go for the jugular. He wants to go for everything. He's matured now in that he allows himself to be pulled back rather than lose everything. My work with him is a very interesting representation to me."

Attorney Skelding is not a Native American, but Jim Shore, who is the closest person to Chief Billie now in the legal department is a blind Seminole who graduated from Stetson law school in 1980.

"The way we got to be lobbyists for the Seminoles was that Osley Saunooke was working with my partner on the business development committee for the Council on Indian Affairs," says Skelding.

"I want to go for everything," says Chief Billie. "When you go for everything, they've got to give you something, or they feel guilty. Bingo tumbleweeded into where every state wanted to do it. You can't go to the state arrogantly though. You have to ask. Every human being should ask for the ultimate.

"We sent Joel Frank to Washington. Joel is very gentlemanly. Joel looks the part. Now that he's been in Washington for three years, Joel wants to come home.

"It's expensive to run our reservations because they're very spread out. I agree with the NRA that every man should be allowed to carry a gun," said the chief.

Because he does not always agree with the *Miami Herald*, Chief Billie started the tribal newspaper, *The Seminole Tribune*, which is published bi-weekly.

"There should be a bounty on all editors," exhorted Billie. "They practice the art of confusion. They don't realize the damage of saying the wrong thing.

"We helped a black fellow named Richardson get out of prison. Then the *Miami Herald* tried to take the credit for it.

"I'm happy the tribe's doing what it's doing," concluded the chief.

The third family in America settled in the historic seaport of St. Augustine. The possibility of a land purchase for the Seminoles there induced Chief Billie to go up and meet Eugenia Genovar.

It was with astonishment that they discovered that Eugenia's ancestor was the one who waved the white flag at Osceola back in 1837. At the Castillio Marcos near St. Augustine, Osceola was induced to surrender along with 80 other Seminoles as they were trying to negotiate the release of King Philip, a second Seminole chief who had been captured earlier.

When her son, Phil Genovar, and his daughter, Sonya, went out to the Indian reservation to meet Chief Billie, James introduced Phil as the man who captured Osceola under a flag of surrender in front of all the Indians.

Sonya said she tried to slink down and pretend she wasn't related to her father, she was so humiliated. Later, she went up in the airplane with the chief. She took over the controls and was playing with the ailerons. Suddenly, the plane went into a sharp nose dive.

"My great great great grandfather captured Osceola and I almost captured the chief. I guess it runs in the family," quipped Sonya.

"He's one of a kind," commented Phil, who spent two days in Washington, D.C. with the chief. "We're lucky there's only one like him." They were there to meet with the Bureau of Land Management and the Bureau of Indian Affairs regarding a possible bingo partnership.

James is always testing, testing, testing. It is his credo. He approaches a problem head-on. He is very open-minded and fair. His sense of justice is absolute.

"He's outrageous," quipped Pat Diamond, his secretary. "He's outrageous from beginning to end."

119

When the chief found out that Indian bones had been found at the Turner's house in Moore Haven he thought about it seriously.

"Where were they found? Maybe they were left from 1926 when a hurricane hit Lake Okeechobee and the lake spilled out like a giant saucer all over the town," said the chief. "They could be one of the people who was drowned in that flood." Deeply curious, James has many theories. James advised us to take them in our room at night and sleep with them, like a true shaman.

Whether due to the bones or not, my husband Thom had a dream that Lake Hicpochee flowed into Big Cypress by way of a canal. When James was told, he confirmed that that used to be true. The old maps of the area showed that canal, which has nowadays been filled in.

One of his theories involves a ten year cycle. He has observed a ten-year cycle on trends in real estate and interest in property. He thinks that somebody loses interest and then later another person rekindles it in a type of business cycle that reoccurs every ten years.

James has a raunchy sense of humor. Dave Vopnford relates how he was bringing his 70 year-old mother and 68 year-old aunt to the Seminole reservation for a visit. Chief Billie offered to cook dinner for them. He threw 30 steaks on the grill to feed six people. He didn't bother setting the table with knives, forks or plates.

He took his knife and just skinned off a piece of one of the steaks, then handed it to Dave's mother to sample.

"If it's not rare enough for you, I'll cut some foreskin off of my dick," joked the chief.

He loves to be the center of attention and usually

commands center stage. At Billie Swamp Safari, he related a story about one of the young men sitting on the porch.

"The first time this fellow went out with a girl he looked in her purse and found this thing. He took it out and put it in his mouth. It was cotton with a string hanging out, so he thought he could smoke it." Everyone laughed at the image, including the guy who was the butt of the joke.

There is a constant striving in the chief to accomplish what he plans for the day.

"He'll tell four or five people to do the same job," says Roy Diamond, director of the Safari.

When the chief is present, everyone hustles. He expects from his employees what he expects of himself.

His son, Micco, owns 500 head of cattle. James and Leslie took friends out to the pasture to show them Micco's herd. Micco aimed the flashlight in the direction of his cows.

Micco is taught Miccosukee at home, but has also picked up Spanish and English. He is a happy boy who smiles and chats with everyone.

Guy LeBree's paintings grace the walls of their home. He has done several works of James, one in which he is shooting a bear with a bow and arrow. There are also family photographs in the living room and kitchen.

James and Leslie love to go deep sea fishing and diving. Leslie has recently gotten her scuba certification. She enjoys roller blading, personal fitness, and speed walking and, of course, shopping. She is a beautiful woman.

121

Leslie has plans to manage a craft business where she will sell native crafts such as bead work and other Seminole jewelry as well as baskets and dolls. She has a twin brother named Wesley from the Immokalee reservation.

"James loves anyone who smiles at him," explains Leslie. There are a slew of people at a long table in their kitchen. James is talking on the phone.

"It's always like this," says Leslie, as she serves us some coffee and tamales. "Take off the wrapper." The tamales are wrapped in corn husks. They are very flavorful.

The chief had an operation in 1991 on his knees because his legs were bowlegged. Robb Tiller dressed up in a gown and went into the operating room with the doctors and nurses. James sent a letter to Robb thanking him for his support. In it, he comments that "The hospital will never be the same."

"That letter means a lot to me," said Robb, who has known Chief Billie for many years. Robb spent a year living in a chickee on the reservation and has come to know the Seminoles quite well.

Robb Tiller remembers when he and Chief Billie organized a city block festival, bringing Seminoles to Tallahassee for "Seminole Indians Salute the State of Florida." The tribe brought cattle, alligators, panthers and snakes native to the reservations. Balloons were arched over the streets in the largest balloon display Tallahassee has ever seen. Hot air balloons were hired to handle the festivities. A demonstration of arts and crafts was conducted.

The tribe took over all the rooms of the Governor's Inn owned by Bud Chiles, the present Governor's son.

The hotel stands across the street from the Florida state capitol building. "Oh my God, the Indians are coming," said a member of the hotel staff.

Seminole children in Tallahassee.

The streets were transformed into "Indiantown" where three chickees were erected to serve the traditional fry bread, Indian burgers, fresh catfish (from the reservation's catfish hatchery) and fresh fruit.

There were eight thousand Floridians celebrating in the streets that day. The Seminoles gave away food and balloons at the day-long celebration. Planes buzzed the

123

top of the capitol building to kick off the salute.

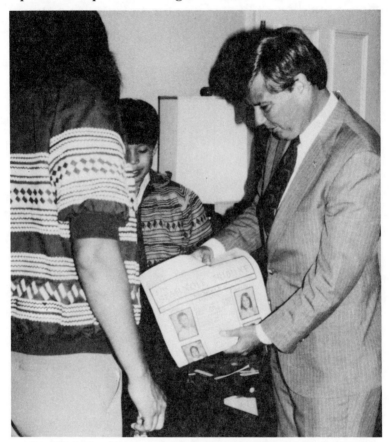

Gov. Bob Graham accepts a copy of the <u>Seminole Tribune</u> from schoolchildren.

Seminole children delivered a copy of *The Seminole Tribune* to the governor, who was then Bob Graham. Dressed in their native clothing, the children presented the paper to Graham personally.

Compliments of the Seminole Tribe, there was an

open bar held at the Governor's Club where James entertained by singing and playing his guitar for the dignitaries. Afterwards, the chief and several helpers swept up the streamers, balloons and other debris so that Tallahassee would be left clean.

James has many people who are jealous of his success. He has helped many tribal members buy trucks. He tries to distribute the wealth of the tribe equitably so as many tribal members as possible will benefit,

The chief's word is as good as a written contract. He is slow to commit to some projects, but once he does, he always follows through with them. The tribe contributes two and a half cents to the Republicans and two and a half cents to the Democrats from each carton of the millions of cartons of cigarettes they sell.

Occasionally, the men and women he deals with change their minds. he is not tolerant when someone charges him more than their original quote. For example, he was angry when his panther video "Ways of the Glades" cost $5,000 more than he had planned to spend. A National Geographic cameraman was hired for the shoot. A deer cage had to be constructed to contain the buck, which pushed the original cost over budget.

James is not someone who carries a grudge. If he is opposed, he overlooks it short term. However, like an elephant, the chief never forgets his friends or his enemies.

"Watch out, he's a rattlesnake," he'll warn.

The origin of a handshake was to show a stranger that you weren't carrying a gun in your right hand. The Indians used the traditional "How" in the same way. Chief Billie wondered how many men who were left-handed were shot by mistake when they held up their gun hand. He pondered these errors in communication.

When James was first elected chief, he got elected by a certain faction in the tribe who expected to be better off because of his leadership. Another faction who didn't vote for him gave him support in his next election because they also wanted to gain from his politics. James learned in Psychology 101 that the first time somebody stands up, he wants to let out his frustrations. This person is venting his opinion and doesn't want to be interrupted. The reaction should not be to smile, but to agree.

He has learned to compromise. Chief Billie uses the same patience he learned while hunting. He listens to everyone, especially the elders of his tribe who still dress in traditional clothes. He is persistent in helping them with their problems. One of the Seminoles needed a new home.

"Give him a stove, a refrigerator, a dishwasher, a garbage disposal, an air conditioner and a hot water heater. Oh yes, and a washer and dryer. I want him to smell good when I meet him again," said James.

On another, he said, "He has five children? I didn't realize he had that many. He's been fooling around a lot. Look him straight in the eye and ask him if that's true."

Another woman needed a halfway house. "Try to get her in somewhere where they don't know her history."

Sometimes help in the form of money is unwelcome.

"I gave a man $300 to help him. It landed him in jail. His wife came to me and asked why I gave him that money," said James. The man used the money to go out and get drunk.

Chief Billie detected some activity on the reservation that was not to his liking. Drugs were finding their way into the hands of some Seminoles.

He knew that the drugs were being flown in by plane. When he heard the familiar hum of an airplane, he got out his gun. He forced them to land and staked them out. He purchased the plane from the DEA for $3,000. But he had a problem. How was he going to keep the drug planes from the reservation for a landing strip? They were bringing in illegal drugs. He asked the sheriff for help. The sheriff told him there was too much area to patrol. He didn't have enough manpower to cover such a wide area.

"Then I'll have to form my own police force," said James. Now the Big Cypress reservation has its own Seminole police force to insure that law and order prevail.

The next time a drug plane landed, he was ready for them. He wanted to shoot the tires, but a policeman shot the pilot as they were trying to escape.

The chief didn't know whether that would be a popular move, but at the next election, he was voted in by a resounding majority.

Seminole display at Bok Tower in Lake Wales, Florida.

Chapter 12

Secrets of His Success

ere are some of the characteristics of this leader that demonstrate his strengths. As chief of the Seminoles, James has power equivalent to the President of the United States on his five reservations.

Say Everything You Have to Say

Since the Seminole language is not a written one, Native Americans use an oral tradition to pass on their heritage from generation to generation. This heritage includes laws, lore, songs, shamanistic medicine, religious rituals and various stories. Seminoles can talk for a long time without any break. This Indian "mindset" should not be interrupted.

Use Persistence

James will move mountains to attain his goals. He began in business by selling alligators for $5 each to tourists as a child. He graduated to building chickees for restaurants. He fights until he achieves his goals. This quality is the trademark of winners in all walks of life.

James rode horses as soon as he could walk. He grew up on Cabbage Palm ranch—an idyllic place for a curious Indian boy who loved climbing trees, riding horses and catching snakes and alligators.

He is a perfectionist. James made an alligator video but wasn't satisfied with it because a piece of canvas was showing in the background. He had the scenes reshot until it was flawless.

If James wants something done, his people feel they can consider it done. Because he has always used persistence, James can't be talked out of achieving his goals.

Don't Be A Sprinter

He is constantly testing, testing, testing. His son, Micco, was riding a pony at the chief's cattle roundup. Suddenly one of the cowboys raised his hat, and the pony startled. Micco slid off and walked around behind the pony. Leslie pulled Micco away so that he wouldn't be kicked. James tested the pony by standing behind him, slapping his rear and pulling on his legs. The pony stood still. "Hmm," thought James. "Maybe he won't kick."

His idea to use bingo as a moneymaker paid off handsomely not only for the Seminoles, but other Indian tribes. James is not a sprinter. He's a marathoner.

Ask for Everything

"Ask for everything when you're up against the government. They'll feel guilty, so they'll have to give you something."

130

James believes in being tough, showing no fear, and going for the jugular. He respects forthrightness.

Take the Most Dramatic Approach

James is a showman. He has a wonderful sense of humor. He loves to see people laugh. His shrewdness is evident when he gets attention in the best manner possible. James figures out what works and what doesn't work.

He uses Federal Express to deliver important messages. This impresses the seriousness of a parcel or letter on the mind of the receiver. *People pay attention!*

He does everything in an original way. A strong sense of personal style sets Chief Billie head and shoulders above the rest. He appears larger-than-life because of this style.

For example, he was flying his helicopter to pick up a golden lab puppy for Micco. Instead of landing near the canal, he asked permission to land in a neighbor's yard. He was closer to the place he wanted to be, thanks to his ingenuity.

Keep Your Friends Close and Your Enemies Closer

Invariably powerful Indian chiefs encounter envy. James deals swiftly and authoritatively with situations he doesn't condone.

As he put it, "You don't want to shoot that tired and skinny deer you feel sorry for. You want to fatten him up a little." James has the ability to defuse his opposition in a whole variety of ways.

In another case, a boy got bitten by an alligator. James smelled the wound to determine that it was healing properly.

Be a Good Role Model

Young people look up to Chief Billie to set a good example for them. The first building James erected on the Big Cypress reservation was a gymnasium. That way the young men would have a place to go to work out.

Several of the employees at Billie Swamp Safari have had personal problems. One had trouble with drugs. Now he is an alligator wrestler, an airboat driver, and a panther keeper. Another had a drinking problem. He is now cured.

Seminole high school students can attend private school if they so choose. The Tribe will pay for their tuition.

A Seminole teen was relating how two men tried to make him drink beer. They were rough with him, as he had a scrape on his nose and some bruises. James listened to him and asked if he would recognize them.

"I just wish they were Seminoles," he said in a threatening voice.

Save What Works, Scrap What Doesn't

First of all, get your work done. "I do my work first after I wake up," says James. His large kitchen is as busy as a boardroom. People are coming and going. The phone is constantly ringing. Plans are thrust in front of him for approval.

James was interested in erecting a Seminole museum. Then he was told it would cost $10 million. He promptly tore down the main chickee and used the cedar posts to construct a restaurant.

Be Self-Sufficient

Learn all you can by observation. James decided to give his son a pony ride. He used a piece of rope to make a halter for the pony. He tied it around the pony's head and presto, he had a bridle and rein.

One night, he, Leslie, and Micco were out checking on their cattle herd. James caught a bird with his bare hands. Micco and Leslie did too.

They have to guard the new calves after they are born or the vultures will peck their eyes out and eat them. They have lost four or five calves already to the vultures.

Understand Other Cultures

This is a multi-cultural society. Now white society is dominant, but that could change. James' heritage is from both Seminole and white culture. Although he was raised as a Seminole, he has had to battle for issues affecting his tribe's future in white courts.

Protect Your Environment

Plant a tree in your community or yard. Observe the birds in your area. Visit the parks and ponds around you

133

to learn about native wildlife. Save injured animals that need help. Be in harmony with your natural surroundings.

Preserve Your Customs

Chief Billie teaches his son, Micco, the Miccosukee language. He is acutely aware how quickly traditions can be lost.

James is a mastermind at running all his enterprises. He is building a museum so that there will be a place to house all the Indian artifacts that the Smithsonian Museum doesn't have room to display. When his building is complete, there will be a permanent record of the Seminoles' heritage for all to see at Big Cypress reservation, as the Smithsonian will donate those artifacts to their rightful owners.

Plan For the Future of the Earth

James is a planner. He gets others motivated. They become excited about doing projects with him. His enthusiasm is contagious.

The Seminoles are setting up a panther preserve to ensure the preservation of the species. As Native Americans, they are keenly aware of what depletion can do to any ecosystem. Upsetting the natural balance can have a devastating effect on the delicate environment of the Everglades.

Balance Out Your Ego

James has spent time trying to balance his ego out. He walked into a movie theater and there was a woman and her son who was about five years old. The mother said to her son, "This is Chief Billie."

The little boy looked up at James and asked his mother, "Chief of what?"

So that was that.

Don't Leave People In Your Wake

Chief Billie always thinks about other people. He is constantly giving them advice that he hopes they will take. His wisdom extends to members of his tribe and all whites that he encounters, too. He is not prejudiced. He would rather have them hop on board than leave them in his wake.

Be Confident

When James was in Vietnam, he had to keep morale up. He remembered that his Seminole medicine man would make a blessing on a cigarette as if it were a protective shield. He passed smoke over his men to protect them in the same manner.

"Any added confidence-making material we'd use," explained the Seminole chief.

Don't Give Me Excuses

There have been people envious of James' successes. He has no use for people who don't keep their word. If James agrees to something, he will stick to it. He expects others to do the same.

"I've never killed anyone. I'd rather keep them around and make them miserable," he threatens.

Pinpoint Your Targets

"I tell people exactly what I'm going to do. If I laugh and giggle a lot, they think I'm fooling. Then when I do it they are surprised, because they thought I was kidding," confides the chief.

James has a lightning-quick mind and a thoroughbred temperament. He can read your expressions to see if you understand what he's telling you.

"I can see you aren't getting what I'm saying, so let me put it another way," he'll tell people.

He delights in shocking people around him with his unorthodox behavior. In restaurants, James will pick up a baked potato whole just to get a reaction. He loves comedians such as Benny Hill, Woody Allen and Charlie Chaplin. He has a great sense of humor and loves to crack jokes.

Keep Your Options Open

Stay open minded. The more irons he has in the fire, the better chance James has of having deals come through. James is a visionary. He can imagine his ideas becoming a reality.

Respect Your Elders

They have lived longer than you and probably have learned a thing or two along the way. Listen to them. James was told by Pete Turner to stay away from drugs. He also was told not to get tattooed "because that's just advertising that you're stupid." James took his advice.

Employ Shamanism

James, as a Seminole Indian, draws from a spiritual knowledge that was taught to him by his grandparents. Shamanism teaches Indians to know the ways of the cattle, the birds, the alligators and all the other creatures in the Everglades. His innate knowledge of animals gives him an instinct he applies to human behavior.

He is a healer. He knows the look of a snake bite. When one of the tribal women was bitten by a pygmy rattler, James diagnosed it and told her to get some vaccine for it. She hadn't seen the snake bite her, and thought it was a fire ant sting until it swelled up her whole foot.

Make Sure You Win

The adage of this Indian chief is to leave nothing to chance. James believes in reconnaissance. He plans out his tactics so that he will achieve the desired outcome in all his many enterprises. It is a lesson he learned from his grandfather. Uncle Sam reinforced it in Vietnam. He carried it with him all his life. It has made him a winner.

Chief Billie waves to cowboys.

Part II

The Seminole World

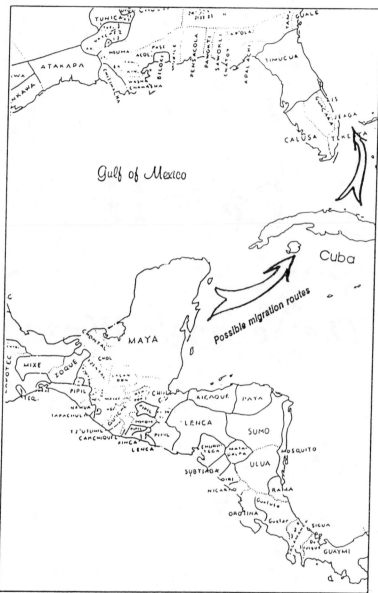

Gulf of Mexico

Cuba

Possible migration routes

The Mayan-Seminole world before Columbus

Chapter 13

Their Origins

Disappearance of the Mayan Indians from Mexico and emergence of the Seminoles in Cuba has led to speculation that a link may exist between the two cultures. Some historians are convinced that the Calusa Indians canoed across the Caribbean, by way of Cuba, from Mexico's Yucatan Peninsula to Florida. One theory hypothesizes that they were swept along by a hurricane, which is certainly possible. In Mexico perhaps overcrowded conditions, or some other reason such as a cruel dictator, forced inhabitants of Uxmal, Tulum and Chichen Itza to set out for a more tolerable climate.

A young Mayan athlete, full of his own success at the games, may have loaded his canoe and paddled for adventure. Instead of retreating to the catacombs under the temple when the Temple of the Winds echoed like a conch shell with the onset of a hurricane at Tulum, this muscular athlete might have decided to set forth to test his strength against the force of the raging tempests.

Let's presume a passing water spout intrigued our mythical hero. He chased it until it evaporated out at sea and, too late, he lost sight of land. Headed for Cuba, he made a successful voyage. Then after a spell there, thirsty for conquest, he set off for the Florida coast. After all, rafters from Cuba arrive daily on the Florida shores. A windsurfer even managed to sail his way from Cuba to Miami.

Tulum, where a Mayan civilization flourished.

Whatever the method, Native Americans were populating this state when the Spanish arrived here in the 1500's from Europe. Florida in the mid-16th century was home to many tribes of Indians. The Calusa were a warlike tribe that inhabited Florida's lower west coast. The Ais lived from Cocoa Beach along the east coast to the St. Lucia River. The Jeaga occupied Palm Beach County and the area of Boca Raton and Deerfield Beach. The Tequesta Indians lived south of Pompano Beach down into several of the Florida keys until 1711, when they were chased off to Cuba by the Seminoles.

Temple of the Winds at Tulum made a sound to warn of approaching hurricanes.

The Mayan Indians of Mexico are a source of great mystery to scholars. Because the Spanish burned all of the books they could find—somewhere around 4,000 existed— the Mayan glyphs are only partially understood.

Discoveries are being made daily in Copan, Honduras, where anthropologists have uncovered rare flint carvings done centuries ago. Flint—the fire stone—was very valuable.

The first similarity between the Seminoles and the Mayans is the chickee. This shelter, built of poles and palm fronds, is reported to be 20 degrees cooler in summertime than the surrounding air. It is rain resilient. Wind will blow through it, preventing damage by hurricanes.

The second factor which makes a strong case for common ancestry is diet. Mayans used to eat corn, beans and squash—nutritionally a completely balanced diet. Seminoles cultivated the same foods, adding pumpkins, in the Everglades.

Third, the mythology of the Mayans, as evidenced by the creatures inlaid in their temples, was based on the animals they knew. At Tulum in Mexico, the Mayans carved out an arch in the form of a serpent. There they performed animal sacrifice in order to please their gods. Other Mayan cities were the sites of human sacrifice. Although the Seminoles stopped short, there are similarities in their shamanistic practices that reflect the sacrificial animals. When Chief Billie killed the panther, it was shared by all the tribal members in a ceremonial banquet.

Fourth, the Seminole clans are headed by animals. The bird, the panther, the snake, the alligator, the deer, the otter, the bear, and the owl were all names of clans. As reflected in their religion and also their burial practices, Mayan Indians used animals in their art and in their lives.

The corn ceremony is the fifth similarity. Celebration of it was the most important Mayan holiday. In Seminole lore, the Green Corn Dance is the equivalent of our New Year's in that it is the time of renewal. Men fast to purify themselves, while women put out their old fires to symbolize the casting out of the old and impure.

The religious beliefs of a society are not static, just as the population is not. There is always an intermingling of faiths, especially with the dominating influence of European cultures on the Indian tribes. In Tulum, Mexico, the main temple is engraved with figures representing the Father, the Son and "nothing" or what Christians would call The Holy Spirit. The zeal to convert the Mayans was fierce. There is a break in the reef offshore where the Spanish boats sailed. When the Indians wanted to signal their friends, they would light torches on top of the temple to show the way, just as our Coast Guard stations built lighthouses as guides to passing vessels. These beacons could be extinguished, however, when the passing ships were Spanish conquistadors in galleons or pirates flying their Jolly Rogers.

The sixth point where they exhibit parallel thinking is on the practice of blood-letting. The ancient Mayans believed that the most sacred of all fluids was blood. The king had a ritual where he pricked the foreskin of his penis then let the blood drip on paper. This paper was burned, as an offering to the gods to be kind to the Mayan people. Seminole ritual involves bloodletting too. When a young man has been disobedient, his skin is scratched as a form of punishment. Scratching is used at the Green Corn Dance as an initiation rite.

The seventh similarity is in their dancing. Mayan dancers used fire to show tribute to their gods. Feather headdresses and foot shakes resembled the costumes of today's Seminole dancers.

Elaborate feathered chief's headdresses were made of golden eagle feathers, the "Cadillac" of bird feathers. Rattles made of tortoise shells communicated the sacred

145

nature of their messages to the Master of them all. Egret plumes graced the garments of the women.

The eighth similarity between the Mayans and the Seminoles is their physical appearance. The Mayans were people with a great deal of physical stamina and strength. This profile fits the average Seminole.

To the Seminoles, the most significant religious event is the Green Corn Dance. The shaman tribal elders congregate to elect officers and dispense justice. This meeting in the early summer takes place when the new crop of corn is ripe. Recently the Seminole tribe purchased a large tract of land in Osceola County. The wooded 2500 acres will be the site for future Green Corn Dances. Another tract was promised to them, explained Chief Billie regarding this acquisition, but the heirs decided to keep it. The Seminole tribal elders authorized another tract to replace it.

Men gather together for the ceremonial lighting of the new fire from a piece of flint that the shaman keeps stored away specifically for this purpose. This fire symbolizes a new beginning of the year. The men sit together and drink the black drink (cassina) to purify themselves as they have been doing for centuries. They hold discussions here.

Women and children come to meet members of other clans. The women cook, clean their homes and watch over the children. The Green Corn Dance is a time for flirting. The young teenage Seminoles find an attractive boy and let him know that they find him desirable. The girls did not kiss him, but demonstrate their affections in other ways.

On the third day, the shaman carries his medicine

bundle into the ceremony. That night he opens it to reveal its contents. At dawn it was closed until the following Green Corn Dance.

The host village sent word to other settlements when the dance would take place. Each clan acted as a welcoming committee to their members from other villages. If temporary housing was needed, everyone pitched in to build enough for visiting clansmen and women.

Fry bread, cooked over an open fire, is popular fare. The bread can be made with pumpkin and is similar to pita bread. Women prepared this food as part of the feasting, after the men and older boys' ritual fast. Other preparations included corn, swamp cabbage, sofki, a drink made with corn, turtle, deer, and wild boar. The women made this feast with the new crops after the kindling of the new fire. The ceremony was attended by all of the clans. After the new fire was lit by the head shaman, the women took coals from the ceremonial fire to their homes. Thus, the Green Corn Dance was considered a new beginning, similar to our celebration of New Year's Eve. If someone had eloped and run away to avoid marrying someone undesirable, they could sneak back in and be forgiven at Green Corn Dance.

The Green Corn Dance had not been performed at Big Cypress during the sixties. In 1962, at the Hollywood Reservation, the Seminole Tribe held its first pow wow. The second annual pow wow was held at Brighton and the third in 1964 at Big Cypress.

The following two years, Hollywood and Brighton reservations each hosted the affair again. Until the 1960's, it had remained entertainment for the Indians only, a day for the clans to spend together. They held athletic events, an arts and crafts show and competition, a "Miss Seminole" contest, a baby contest, a judging of the finest traditional and modern applications of the sewn patchwork strips and a big banquet for all.

Long ago in Mexico, the competitive ball games that the Mayan warriors played were ruthless contests of superiority that are too bloody for society today. There are traces of these competitions in the drag races that were popular in the 1950's, the sports of basketball and football, and the team school events that many high school students enjoy. Modern-day Seminoles ride airboats, motorcycles, horses, pick-up trucks, and swamp buggies for their own sport. "Mudding" is a track where vehicles are taken for a romp through the wet dirt.

Each culture has traditions that are dear to them. The history of the Seminoles is rich in colorful folklore which gives each Indian a sense of his past and a heritage to pass along to his children.

Although each generation has its own trends, the tradition of the Green Corn Dance has survived to this day. Now that land has been purchased by Chief Billie specifically for this unique Seminole event, it seems certain the Green Corn Dance will be perpetuated as part of the religious life of the Seminole Tribe of Florida. Their elders have fostered a respect for this tradition. Through their adherence to this tradition, the Seminole ways will survive.

Chapter 14

The Clans

J ust as the Everglades provided motherly nurturing and sustenance to the Seminoles, clan membership can be equated to a protective father. Every member of the tribe knows his clan. There was even a clan invented to absorb non-Indian women into the system called "Big Town."

In the study done of the Big Cypress community in 1970, Merwyn S. Garbarino observed, "There are only seven clans represented at Big Cypress now: Tiger, Wind, Bird, Otter, Bear, Wolf and Big Town. 'Tiger' is really an incorrect translation of the Miccosukee word which means puma, an animal native to the southeastern area, for the tiger is an Asiatic or African animal."

At that time, two of the clans were becoming extinct. The only wolf was an old man. Since the children retained the clan of their genetic mothers under all circumstances, adoption to prevent clan extinction was impossible. Another clan in danger of extinction was the Bear, which had only three old men and one childless old woman left.

Election and not inheritance is the accepted form of tribal leadership now, although in the past, the head of the tribe came from the Snake clan at Big Cypress. But even though their importance is diminishing, the clans among the Seminoles have played a significant dynastic role in their history. The two clans that provided leadership were the Tiger and Wind clans. At the Green Corn Dance, the Indians sat in two groups around the fire. Members of the head clans sat opposite each other. These individuals were addressed by the other clan members as mother's brother.

There is no longer any clan head in this community. The need for this role has largely been replaced since the Seminoles started living on reservations. The ceremonial Green Corn Dance was organized along clan lines, but in 1970 there was no dance held on the Big Cypress reservation.

The main function of the clan, then, was to regulate marriage, for clan exogamy is still observed. To marry within one's own clan is thought to be bad, even though there were four intra clan marriages in the community at the time of Garbarino's study. The people in these marriages are not outcasts in any way, but everyone knows that they have broken clan exogamy, and it is spoken of very disapprovingly.

The young people are not as convinced of the validity of the clan manner of choosing a mate as are the elders. It seems that the clan system of allowing some marriages and forbidding others was a primitive way of preventing inbreeding.

Chief Billie is a member of the Bird clan. The clan members do not claim to be descendants of the animal though, nor is there any sort of taboo against killing or eating the animal.

Most people are proud of their clan membership. One

woman Garbarino asked said: "I have always been proud to be a Bird because I think it is better than a Tiger or Otter or something. Birds are nice. But I don't think anyone else thinks that way. I guess everyone thinks his own clan is best. I never heard that anyone is ashamed of his clan."

The individualistic ways of the Seminole Indians have stood them in good stead. Their songs are really fables that show young children how to live, much like nursery rhymes and counting songs in white culture.

Like societies such as the Hawaiians that depended on an oral tradition, some of the Seminole lore has been lost, since it was passed down through the clan elders. Also, the Seminole language has been incorrectly translated. However, enough of the rich cultural heritage has been preserved in English, thanks to some historians interested in the Indian way of life.

The clan protected the family unit of the Seminole from harm by setting up laws enforced by the clan. It also gave the individual a name and a lineage.

The dead bodies of ancestors used to be put up on pedestals by their clansmen. These bodies were watched over by someone of lesser birth, such as a slave. If an animal stole one of these bodies, the person responsible for watching over it could be put to death for his negligence. This happened when a wolf stole a child of a chief's dead body that Ortez, a white man, was supposed to be protecting. Ortez shot the wolf with an arrow and killed it. Otherwise he would have been put to death.

In my own family, the dead were dug up and moved along with the living members of the family out on eastern Long Island. This curious practice may also have been a custom of the Seminoles.

The Seminole form of discipline was a unique punishment and a humiliating one. The elders of the clan would invoke scratching with a sharp object, such as an animal claw, to reprimand the delinquent. The marks would leave scars for all the members of the clan to see.

There were also occasional decrees of death if the crime warranted it. Lesser offenses such as incest or adultery were exonerated with the cutting off of the offender's nose, ears or lips. The clan leader decided what penalty would be enforced.

Tribal councils were held every year at the Green corn Dance in the spring. Shamans were frequently elevated to leadership positions because of their vast knowledge of all kinds of natural, and supernatural, phenomena. Misfortune was blamed on the chief. Sometimes a new chief would be elected if the tribe suffered under their ruler.

Seminoles were scattered into towns during the three wars they had to endure. Patterns that they had maintained historically often had to be abandoned, so often what was true on one reservation wasn't the custom on another. For example, Big Cypress had a Tiger clan, whereas Immokalee, Brighton and Hollywood had a Panther clan.

The Everglades sheltered the Seminoles when the U.S. Government was trying to remove them from Florida. This intention to ferret out the Indians fostered a distrust of the white man that has lasted to this day. Chief Billie is credited with a refusal to give up their unique ways, while at the same time winning at the white man's game.

At Big Cypress, the Indians used to refer to themselves as Miccosukee first of all. Although there were also Creek Indians living there, they primarily lived at the Brighton reservation. Today they all call themselves Seminoles.

Some traditions are derived from the Creek. The *Micco* was the equivalent of the mayor today. He was the leader the town. In war time, a war chief who had had experience in battle was chosen to lead the tribe. The Micco always came from one clan and the war chief from another.

The two clans that produced these vital positions—the Alligator and the Snake—are both gone at Big Cypress now. All the tradition of clan inheritance was annihilated after the Third Seminole War around 1858.

The function of the clans was weakened when reservation life replaced swamp life for the Seminoles. Now a democratic process of election became the way to elevate a person to power in the tribe. At the insistence of the people, the office holders mediated on behalf of their constituents. For one thing, they didn't trust the agency. For another, they were not used to dealing with groups of people except within their own families or clans.

Suspicious of the white men trying to teach them cattle raising, the Indians had different ideas of stock raising than their white counterparts. Naturally, this gave way to misunderstandings.

In summary, the function of the clan is still an important one to Native Americans from many tribes. It differentiates a member from the white community, where the closest equivalent is that of a Godfather, and it is a source of pride to the individual.

Ian holds alligator's mouth shut.

Chapter 15

Their Leaders

C hief James Billie is the latest in an illustrious tradition of tough Seminole warriors. If not for two crucial factors, the two Seminole tribes that exist today, one in Florida and one in Oklahoma, may long ago have become one Oklahoma tribe.

The first factor was the Everglades. The steamy, un-mapped, impenetrable mosquito-infested wet hot hammocks and swamps that the Seminoles called home were anything but inviting to battle-wise Indian fighters used to milder conditions.

Military leaders such as Winfield Scott and Duncan Clinch, with fine military records in clashes against Native Americans in other places, would fail utterly in Florida. They were defeated when it came to handling their men and supplies in the harsh Florida environment. Army procedure said to saturate the targeted area with militia, regular soldiers and Native American guides, build forts, then attack the villages. However, this strategy proved ineffective against the Florida Everglades Seminoles. These Indians had devised guerrilla warfare of their own. They had horses and slaves from trading with the Spanish, gunpowder from the agency, and supplies from Cuba.

The second, more important factor that cemented the Seminole resolve to stay was the war Chief Osceola's death in prison. After eight years of fighting, Osceola, known as the "Snake of the Everglades," because he was so elusive, was tired of war and short of food. He believed General Thomas Jesup had called him in to St. Augustine under a white flag of truce to discuss a treaty with him. Instead, Osceola was tricked into coming in and savagely thrown into prison.

Florida was the only state to have five flags flown over it: the Spanish, British, French, Confederate and United States. During the first and second Seminole Wars the British became allies of the Seminoles. They traded furs for guns and ammunition.

The Seminoles' history of resistance to relocation was unrelenting. Led by war Chief Osceola, the Indians learned ambush techniques against the army. Although he was not in favor of raids on plantations, small bands of Seminoles terrorized settlers and burned their homes. The Second Seminole war cost 1,521 American soldiers and nearly 100 civilians their lives. Millions of dollars went to support the seven-year campaign.

All of the military might was futile. The Seminoles were not going to be ousted, whatever the cost. They considered this land their home. Words and armies and promises couldn't sway them.

Regarding the prospect of relocation beyond the Mississippi River, the words of Chief Jumper ring out clearly. "Your talk is a good one, but my people cannot say they will go. We are not willing to do so. If their tongues say yes, their hearts cry no, and call them liars."

The history of the Seminoles in Florida has always

been turbulent. The First Seminole War began in November, 1817, when Florida was still owned by Spain. Not until February, 1921 did the United States purchase Florida from Spain. With it went the responsibility for over 5,000 Seminoles.

Settlers bristled at the Seminole practice of harboring their slaves. Indians and settlers both stole livestock, burned houses and murdered each other in disputes over territory. An English trader named Arbuthnot related in his journal how the Creeks and Seminoles were ill treated by the English and robbed by the Americans. Arbuthnot kept his goods in the Spanish fort at St. Marks where he had 500 deer skins, dry goods, dishes, lead, molasses, gun powder, sugar and forty barrels of salt.

Andrew Jackson, learning of the uprisings, gave Major David E. Twiggs, commander of Fort Scott, permission to remove the Red Sticks, led by Neamathla, presumably because they were living on U.S. territory. This policy of removal towards all Native Americans was to become Jackson's brutal method of dealing with "the Indian problem."

Twiggs, following orders, led 250 men to Fowltown on an all-night march. Most Seminoles escaped into the swamps, but four men and one woman were slain.

In retaliation, a boat from Fort Scott was fired upon by the Indians on November 30, 1817. Of the over 50 people aboard, six men jumped overboard and escaped to Fort Scott to report the attack. All but 13 people were killed in the boat commanded by Lieutenant Robert W. Scott.

Historically, the Seminoles befriended runaway slaves. Osceola, the Seminole war chief, was a man of enormous strength. Word spread among blacks that they were much better off with the Seminole Indians than they were with white plantation owners. However, the greedy plantation owners wanted the Florida land that the Indians inhabited. A cruel governmental policy was thought up by Jackson: remove the Indians from Florida and force them to rejoin their Creek relatives west of the Mississippi.

In 1832, after viewing the land, several Seminole leaders signed the Treaty of Fort Gibson, although there is some dispute about whether the intent was to agree to move. Micanopy was never in favor of relocating to Arkansas. Some Seminoles were ready to leave Florida, but they were outvoted by the ones wanting to remain. The battle was over possession of Florida land. The Second Seminole War from 1835-1842 was a costly one for the government. From $30 million to $40 million was spent to try to coerce the many bands of Seminoles to move West.

Osceola was totally against leaving Florida. He killed Charley Emathla upon learning that he had sold his cattle in preparation for departure. When word spread of this, Seminoles were discouraged from selling any more cattle.

The allegiance of many blacks to Osceola was caused by raids by white slave traders who took families of blacks indiscriminately and sold them into slavery. Abraham, a black interpreter for Osceola, had his freedom to lose while the Seminoles had their land in the Everglades to lose.

Abraham was a formidable ally, recruiting slaves from the sugar plantations in central Florida while their owners were away or asleep. He offered freedom to them if they would help fight with Osceola against the whites. Many found this offer too good to refuse.

Osceola, which means "shouts when drinking the black drink," would rather have died than move to Arkansas. When he was asked to sign a treaty agreeing to move, he stabbed his hunting knife through it and declared, "This is the only way I sign."

Wiley Thompson, the Indian agent, was scalped by Osceola near Fort King. A war party of 60 warriors led by Chief Osceola ambushed him and Lieutenant Constantine Smith, Second Artillery. Five other whites were also killed.

On December 28, 1835, the same day as Osceola was attacking Thompson, Alligator, another Seminole leader, and Chief Jumper were planning to ambush the 108 member Fourth Infantry army. The first U.S. troops to arrive in Florida, the men were marching to Fort Brooke. In what was to be called the *Dade Massacre*, Seminole warriors, led by Micanopy who fired the first shot, appeared from behind trees, aimed their rifles, and killed half the white men immediately.

As the Indians were returning to their camp supposing all were dead, a brave came up and told the Seminoles that the white men who were still alive were building a fort of logs. They were trying to protect themselves. They had guns, but no powder. They had a cannon, but the balls sailed over the Indians who returned to finish them off.

After talking to them in English, the blacks put to death the three remaining white men. One of the white men "seized an Indian, Jumper's cousin, took away his rifle, and with one blow with it beat his brains, then ran some distance up the road; but two Indians on horseback overtook him, who, afraid to approach, stood at a distance and shot him down. The firing had ceased, and all was quiet when we returned to the swamp about noon."

The white men were not as attuned to the sounds of the swamps as the Seminoles. The ability to hear danger certainly contributed to the Seminoles' determination to stay in the Everglades despite all the efforts of the white government to coerce them to go to Oklahoma. Since drums would give away their location, the Seminoles used shakers to communicate their positions.

Also contributing to their survival was their varied diet. At age 11, Billy Bowlegs III from the Snake clan of royalty, shot his first deer with a muzzle-loading shotgun five miles from his home on the Brighton reservation. Otter and fish were abundant in this sportsman's paradise at the turn of the century.

One day Cofehatke, meaning Rabbit, killed and skinned out nine deer. He recalled during a month that he had killed 53 deer. Billy Bowlegs III hunted all over South Florida. He sold meat to the steamboat captains who cruised up and down the Caloosahatchee and Kissimmee Rivers. He was an experienced alligator hunter. He could make noises like an alligator called "grunting up a gator" and won a world championship at Moore Haven for turkey calling.

Billy was hired as a guide by nationally known sportsmen in the early era of Florida. The list of people he led included author Charles B. Corey, Henry Flagler and his guests, H. B. Plant and his guests, and others. He taught himself English by copying the labels on cans in trading posts with a stick and some berry juice.

Billy Bowlegs had an ox that he rode and trained to

pull a sled. After taking his ox, which wore a bell, to the outskirts of Ft. Pierce once, Billy turned him loose to graze and boarded a train for Orlando. In Orlando he purchased a new one-horse wagon, painted green with red wheels, for fifty dollars from Mr. Avery, the manufacturer. Returning to Ft. Pierce, he went after his ox and yoked him up to his new wagon. Billy said, "I was then *Mr.* Billy Bowlegs."

He was a tall Indian, standing 6'2" and straight as an arrow. He was dark complexioned, eagle-eyed and he eventually wore a neatly trimmed mustache that turned white with age. Billy's vocabulary contained about two hundred English words, but he made good use of them. There were no curse words in the Seminole language, and though he heard them often, Billy never used any of the white man's vulgarities.

Chief Billie is a hunter in the tradition of these great Seminole hunters. He is concerned with setting a good example to the next generation of Seminole warriors.

When James was in Vietnam, Betty Mae Jumper was elected chief. Serving from 1966 to 1970, Chief Betty Mae got to know President Richard Nixon well. He took her and eight other Indian chiefs to Alaska as well as other reservations around the country. Chief Betty Mae, born Betty Mae Tiger, used to discuss Indian affairs with President Nixon over coffee. Her husband was a descendant of Chief Jumper who led the Dade massacre. Betty Mae is the editor of the newspaper published by the tribe, *The Seminole Tribune.*

In her own words, Betty Mae declared, "I've done everything." Writer, teacher, singer, storyteller and Seminole chief, Betty Mae also wrestled alligators when

161

her husband was late for work. She was the first Seminole to graduate from high school, starting at 14 and graduating at 22.

For Chief Billie's birthday one year, she complied a book called "This is Your Life: Chief Jim Billie." Patterned after the TV show of that name, it chronicled his career.

Seminole dolls in patchwork clothes

Chapter 16

Their Crafts

y far the most popular items with tourists are the lovable Seminole dolls. Made of palmetto fiber, these dolls have endeared themselves to many a Florida visitor. The colorful patchwork clothes in a rainbow of colors has attracted a following for this Native American craft. Available in a variety of sizes, these homemade dolls are still being made today.

There are several patchwork designs that have been carried on since the advent of the sewing machine around 1920 for the tribe. These symbols include 1: rain, 2: lightning-thunder, 3: fire, 4: broken arrow, 5: man on horse, 6: bird, 7: four directions, 8: crawfish, 9: tree, 10: diamondback rattlesnake, 11: disagree, and 12: bones.

Women continue to sew the traditional clothing for sale to tourists and collectors. Although the modern everyday clothing has crept into the tribal ways, Seminole patchwork is still worn for ceremonial occasions such as pow wows and the Green Corn Dance.

The young Seminole girl in the photo on the next page sports a long dress that is worn by the children today. She is showing off her kitten. She was interested in lipstick and nail polish. She asked to use my camera to take my picture. She wanted me to put lipstick on her so I complied. Then she put some on me. Some Seminole women are shy, but this young lady was very friendly and eager to talk to us. Her mother was working in the office of Billie Swamp Safari while her daughter kept us entertained.

Seminole girl lets my husband, Thom, pet her kitten.

Baskets were a part of everyday life for the Seminole. They were handy for gathering berries. Constructed of cane, reed or straw, they were lightweight and could be transported easily. Clay was smeared inside and allowed to dry to keep bugs away from the food.

The Seminoles also made attractive jewelry and head ornaments of feathers. Silver, both plain and with cut-out designs, was popular in the form of turban decoration, arm bands, crescent-shaped breast plates and necklaces. Many types of animal claws were used as pendants. Alligator teeth were carved in the form of birds and carried for good luck. Shells and bone were carved into animal shapes. Eagle feathers and turkey feathers were used for ceremonial dance costumes. Anklets were also worn.

Headdresses were sewn from beads and dyed feathers. They were elaborately decorated and very festive. Medicine pouches were stitched from deerskin which carried the shaman's potions.

Pottery was a useful craft because pots were necessary for cooking, eating and storage. Designs were embossed on the sides before the clay was baked which made them permanently part of the piece.

Wooden bows and arrows, spoons and ladles were carved from cypress and oak trees. Large wooden mortar and pestles were whittled for grinding corn.

Dugout canoes were very necessary to the Seminoles for transportation around their watery territory. The canoes were made from cypress trunks. They chose this type of wood because it was easy to carve and buoyant. The Indian men built a fire on the tree, then scraped out the charred ash with axes and picks. A push pole was the normal way of propelling the canoe, but occasionally the boat was fitted with mast and sail.

Woodcarving was a way to earn income by selling souvenirs to tourists at places along the main roads in Florida. Seminoles sold cypress knees and carved wooden alligators in front of a paddle wheeler that plied the intracoastal waterway from Lake Worth. Painted spoons, canoes, and tomahawks were part of the tourist trade items that the Seminoles carved from wood. Adept at trading, the Seminoles of Florida lived simply by selling their carvings to visitors who comprised a steady market. From Tampa to Miami, the Indians' wooden wares were readily available as gifts for people back North.

Spears were fashioned for stabbing turtles, which they enjoy eating to this day. They also invented a "gopher puller" made of a flexible vine with a wire hook at the end that was used to extract the large gopher tortoise from his hiding place under ground. Seminoles boil up turtle soup made from gopher turtles.

The chickee is an enclosed area or hut where the Seminoles lived. The roof is thatched with palmetto leaves in a distinctive pattern. The builder can be identified by his style of roof. These chickees have become popular all over Florida and are often called "tiki bars" or "chickee bars."

One was recently blown away at the dockside restaurant in Ft. Pierce by Hurricane Andrew. The roof is built about 30' high so that it will not catch fire from the cooking logs placed in a pattern of four, representing the four winds.

In Seminole villages, there were several chickees for different purposes. One was for cooking, another for sleeping, another for entertaining and one a distance away called the "baby house" where a pregnant mother would go to give birth.

If someone dies, their chickee is left up as a kind of memorial to them. All Seminole families on Big Cypress have chickees next to their cement block houses. Some have washing machines in them. Others are used for outdoor cooking in the traditional Seminole way.

Chapter 17

Their Environment

"Seminole teenagers can choose whether they want to attend public or private school," said Gloria Wilson, who runs a teen leadership group on the Hollywood reservation. "The Seminole Tribe will pay their tuition."

According to Winifred Tiger, retired Director of Education for the Seminoles, "Historically the Seminoles had problems entering public school. They were treated like blacks and were not welcome in the Florida schools until 1957 when they incorporated. The federal government funded a Cherokee boarding school in Cherokee, North Carolina in the 1930's. The tribes that sent children there were the Choctaws from Mississippi, the Chitimachee from Louisiana, the Seminoles from Florida and the Cherokees of North Carolina."

"Sequoia wrote the first alphabet. His newspaper was called *Talking Leaves*. The Cherokees have always been interested in education," said Tiger, a Cherokee tribal member herself.

‐ Winifred's husband, Howard Tiger, was the first Seminole to volunteer for the armed forces. He was a marine involved in the Iwo Jima invasion. She and Howard were married in 1946 after the war.

167

Up until 1924, Indians weren't considered citizens of the United States. "Everyone who came into the United States was granted citizenship, but Native Americans who were already here weren't allowed to vote until 1924. We didn't have to register and weren't drafted, but my husband volunteered," said Tiger.

Moses Jumper joined the navy later and was the second Seminole enlistee. He was the husband of Betty Mae Jumper.

"We brought James back from Cherokee, North Carolina when he was 4 or 5 years old. He was coming back with us to the Dania reservation, which later changed its name to Hollywood from his aunt's house in North Carolina."

"Any tribal person who is at least 1/4 Indian can be sent to college and the federal government will pay for it," said Tiger.

Since the Seminoles speak either Miccosukee or Muskogee (Creek), there was much history lost because their tradition was an oral one. Gathering information is significant, however, to preserve the genealogies for future generations. Native Americans are a fascinating part of our country's past. Learning about their society will provide insight into a people who have a symbiotic relationship with nature. In the case of the Seminoles, they are at home in their Everglades swamp.

There are 14 laws in the Seminole judicial system. They are similar to the 10 Commandments, and govern the actions of the members of the tribe. One is to respect your elders. Others are concerned with the taboos associated with the clans. There is the custom that at the cemetery you shouldn't step on a grave. There is a taboo that prevents a Seminole from looking at someone who has died. Another law says that if you have broken bones, don't go into a cemetery or evil spirits will get you. Another law dictates that if a fellow clan member dies, that clan group must go on a fast.

Joel Frank, a tribal member whose parents worked at the Seminole tourist attractions, lived down in Miami. After that he attended West Palm Beach elementary school in Highland Park. He calls himself "a product of the new thinking."

"Before the termination period, there was Indian resistance by our elders to keep us out of white schools. The Indians were treated a half step above blacks then. Therefore there were a lot of uncertainties."

In the 50's and 60's Seminoles also did not go to white hospitals. The Bureau of Indian Affairs provided a health service and then the Department of Health, Education and Welfare of the government took over and they were put under the Public Health Service.

"It was during 1954-56 when our tribal leaders decided that we should get acquainted with our neighbors so we were able to survive in the dominant world," said Frank.

Out at Tamiami Trail, there was resistance to going to school. Miccosukee Indians fought in court. When he was 12 years old, Billy Cypress litigated the right of the Indians to educate themselves. The Miccosukees have their own school on the reservation. They are not bound under the Compulsory Education Act. They can either be educated at home like the Amish or they don't have to do anything. They have the choice.

"Sometimes they had trouble catching us," jokes

Frank. His allusion is to James' reluctance to attend elementary school as a boy.

Health was under the B.I.A. until 1957. The Sayler Act was named after the legislator who introduced the bill. Health Services was in charge until 1964 when Indian Health was put under the Department of Health, Education and Welfare. Six or seven years ago it was put under Human Health Services. Trahill, an Indian, will be head of Health if he is confirmed by the Senate.

The Secretary of IHS is a cabinet appointee. Even though IHS has not reached the same level as the B.I.A., which has an assistant secretary, Indians are slowly moving up. Now the Director of Indian Health Services must be confirmed by the Senate, whereas before this wasn't necessary.

Now, Indian children have opportunities undreamed of back in the days when they had to go to North Carolina for an education. Laura Mae Osceola's granddaughter, Councilman Max Osceola's daughter, Melissa Osceola goes to Pinecrest, an exclusive high school in Boca Raton. She recently came back from a trip to Paris and presented the chief with a bottle of French wine. Chief James Billie wants his tribal members to have the best there is in the field of education.

**

SEMINOLE DEER HUNTING PRAYER

"I remember my grandfather used to say a prayer before he went hunting. As a boy I thought it was some mumbo jumbo, but now I know it was to the Creator," said Chief Billie. "He would say the following prayer:

I'm looking for something with horns
I'm looking for something with hide
I'm looking for something with white under his belly
I want him standing far off in a clearing

I'm sorry to kill you
I'll use every part of you
I'll use your hide for clothing
I'll use your meat for food
I'll use as much of your entrails as I can
I'll melt your hooves down
    May your kind prosper forever.

SEMINOLE WORDS

Words in Miccosukee ending in "ee" are connected to water.

Okeechobee	means	"big water"
Kissimmee	"	"winding water"
Pahayokee	"	"grassy water"
Wampee	"	"pickerel weed" (a water plant)
Hatchee	"	"river"
Weeki Wachee	"	"a small spring"

Other words are the following:

ee-chno	is a	deer
ya-laahe	is an	orange
ha-no-li	is	domesticated fruit
o-pa	is an	owl
hen-le	is a	squirrel
sho-ke	is a	pig
laa-le	is a	fish
yok-che	is a	turtle
chen-le	is a	snake
ke-hay-ke	is a	hawk
nak-ne	is a	man
coo-wah-chobee	is a	big cat
hul-pa-te cho-bee	is an	alligator
Aripeka	is a	town named for a Seminole chief
Elfers	is the	"hunting grounds"
Wacasassa	is the	cattle place
Thonotosassa	is the	flint place
Chassahowitza	is a	hanging pumpkin

Part III

*Chief Billie Leads the
Seminoles into
the 21st Century*

Reception chickee

Aerial view of Billie Swap Safari under construction

Chapter 18

Billie Swamp Safari

$\mathcal{I}$ntimately involved with the day-to-day running of the wilderness adventure park, the chief sketched out a diagram of a chickee for his builder. "It had better be 30 feet high or it'll catch on fire," he instructed the carpenter. The spokes of the roof spun out in a wheel. He sectioned it into 16 pieces. He knew this pattern well, since he had organized a chickee building business when he returned from Vietnam.

Florida Trend magazine rated the Billie Swamp Water Cafe a top Blue Highway eatery. Their review said that James Billie runs Florida's best out-of-the-way restaurant. The cafe serves a buffet every day along with a menu consisting of frog legs, swamp baskets of shrimp, chicken, or fish, hamburgers served on Indian bread—a delicious fried bread specialty of the Seminoles, similar to pita bread in flavor. The restaurant is a gathering place for the Cattleman's Association. There is a stage in the corner where James may pick up his guitar to entertain the guests.

Outside, animals are everywhere. A herd of buffalo roam the corral leading up to the entrance. Panthers in cages purr when stroked through the bars, while larger ones stare down from a perch in the trees. Cockatiels sing in a nearby aviary. Saddled horses stand ready to give rides around the meandering wooded trails.

With this enterprise, Chief Billie has the best interests of his tribe at heart. Responsible for a vast amount of Everglades acreage, he runs his reservations with a fear motivation and an iron hand. Discipline he learned in the infantry is applied to his bringing out the best in the people he employs. His ability to motivate others is a major asset in the chief's management style.

An alligator pit is located adjacent to the Swamp Water Cafe. The four foot wall surrounds the reptiles: five alligators, several turtles, and two crocodiles. At feeding time, one gator grabbed a rack of ribs that was so large it couldn't fit down his throat. He tried several times, unsuccessfully, to swallow it. A small gator latched onto the ribs. He then proceeded to spin himself over and over, around and around like a corkscrew until a piece of the ribs tore off. In this way, they split their dinner.

Sitting in one of the chickees overlooking the canal, Swamp Owl shared his large collection of Indian clothing, guns, arrows, carved alligator teeth, and stories. He held up each item while the sun set behind him. The atmosphere brought to life the days when Seminoles were at war with the whites who were trying to relocate them to Arkansas. Alligators played a key role in their survival. The women would tie the live gator up until it was butchered.

"Everybody wants to be a chief and nobody wants to be an Indian. Me, I just want to be an Indian," observed Paul Simmons, an alligator wrestler at the park. He also conducts sunset swamp tours in the dune buggy. The sawgrass and pine hammocks are home to wildlife, mostly nocturnal, which visitors can observe in their natural surroundings. Big Cypress is 2,000 acres of pasture, woodland, and swamp.

Billie Swamp Safari is an ideal campground. Rita Dion, who runs a program for underprivileged children in Vero Beach, was impressed with the facilities. "The children each have a volunteer with them when we go camping for the weekend. We were thinking of going to Orlando, but this is much more educational for them. They can learn about the Indians and see live alligators. There are horseback rides and airboat rides. It'll be a great experience for us all."

Bob Dion was watching the Indian children play in the water. They were trying to launch their canoes. The interaction of the visitors with the children is spontaneous. When the canoe rolled over, the Indian children laughed with glee. After touring the grounds, we stopped by the Swamp Water Cafe for the barbecued rib buffet.

This time the chief was busy supervising the videotaping of the alligator pit with a cameraman and some Japanese businessmen. He motioned for us to be quiet.

On another occasion, the alligator pit was the scene of an alligator wrestling show. There were three men together in the pit. Swamp Owl was announcing the proceedings. A group of German tourists surrounded the pit with cameras poised. The tour leader translated Swamp Owl's words into German.

Controlling alligators is not an exact science. One alligator which measured twelve feet, eight inches, was added to the pen. The next morning tracks showed that he had climbed right over the wall and escaped into the canal. Some of the alligator wrestlers have been bitten by

177

the dangerous reptiles, even though they try to plan the shows after the alligators have been fed. Swamp Owl rescued one young Seminole by grabbing the alligator by his ears and making him open his jaws.

James strums while Leif, Leslie and Micco keep their eyes on the alligator.

Still, the excitement is contagious. What makes Billie Swamp Safari unique is the outdoor atmosphere and the lack of structured activities. It is a memorable adventure for children and adults alike.

"Chief Billie is wonderful with children," states Barbara Vopnford, wife of Dave Vopnford, who owns the RV camp-ground at Big Cypress and is President of

Thousand Adventures, Inc. When their son Leif visited the reservation, he went back to Nebraska with stories of rolling around with alligators. He earned the Indian name of "gator poop" from James.

Well, Leif's school friends were skeptical. After all, they had never seen Indians or alligators before. Word got back to Chief Billie that they were calling Leif a liar. A Lear jet was sent down to pick up the Seminole chief. He brought along a six foot alligator for good measure. An assembly was called for all the school children and Leif's picture wearing his Seminole jacket was on the front page of the local Nebraska newspaper accompanied by Chief Billie, his tribes-men and the alligator, which found a temporary home in the Vopnford's bathtub.

Billie Swamp Safari is a flurry of bird life. Wood storks fish in the swamps. Eagles hover overhead, soaring in the gentle winds that caress the reservation. White egrets follow robot-like after the cattle to pick up insects to ingest. One pond has a pine tree on its bank that fills up with white doves that look like peace ornaments on a Christmas tree. Buzzards wait on fence posts to scavenge turtles, rabbits, and snakes killed by passing cars. Crows canvas the landscape for food. Swamp owls hoot a warning to field mice. Seminoles believe the niche they fill is all part of the Breathmaker's plan.

Big Cypress reservation is about 45 minutes from Moore Haven on Lake Okeechobee. The lake is the biggest bass fishing lake in the country. One can imagine the Seminoles back in the days of Billy Bowlegs III when the wild game was plentiful, leading white huntsmen around the backwoods.

The attraction to Billie Swamp Safari is that one is transported back in time to the days when animals

179

roamed freely around the reservation. Bear, wolf, deer, wild turkeys, otter, fish, boar and, of course, alligators populated the land. Hunters never went hungry. Sport fishing was a way of life.

"I'm a showman," concedes the extroverted chief. "I was brought up in a tourist attraction." The Safari contains an entertainment chickee with wooden bleachers and a stage for performances. Music acts are booked into it. The palm frond roof protects the audience from a sudden afternoon thunderstorm. Billie Swamp Safari provides a tourist attraction conveniently right next door to one of his homes. He has built a runway on the reservation so that it can accommodate his helicopters and airplanes.

James' latest addition to his fleet is an Aero Commander jet that has televisions for every seat. It holds 14 passengers. When it was landing, Seminole cattle had gotten loose on the runway, but the jet avoided them and came down smoothly.

"He goes in 50 directions at once," observed Bert Crowell, President of Renegade Boat Company. "He's a controversial character," said Bert. He has orders to build ten Indian canoes for Billie Swamp Safari. Bert, a resident of Moore Haven, is an expert bass fisherman. His company is marketing a line of bass boats named Micco, in honor of the Seminole chief's son. Bert has built a bass boat for James.

Construction has begun on the multi-million dollar Ah-tha-thi-ki Museum project. The name is Miccosukee for "A place to learn, a place to remember." This museum will add a cultural dimension to the wilderness experience of Billie Swamp Safari. This Seminole museum is being built to educate the public about the

Seminole customs and language. Since Miccosukee is a spoken language, oral legends handed down through the clans have not bee interpreted into English. In order to preserve this rich heritage, the museum will contain an oral history section.

The buildings will be housed on a 60-acre site about a mile down the road from Billie Swamp Safari and across the street from the airstrip. There will be a number of ponds, docks and water trails in the center of the site. A wildlife exhibit, fish camp exhibit, airboat exhibit and canoe exhibit will be part of the display open to visitors. Ceremonial grounds will also be featured. A long house and a hunting camp will be built to show them as centers of Indian activity.

The pride of the Seminole people will be reflected in their history going back to the three Seminole Wars. Building number one will be devoted to Seminole Heritage. The library and archives will comprise part of this main facility. The second building is earmarked for administration and education. An archivist will coordinate the revolving exhibits at the museum, along with the lectures and audiovisual demonstrations. The auditorium, gallery and dining rooms will comprise the third building. The auditorium will be available for unlimited arrangements for dance, plays, forums and lectures.

A fourth building is slated to be for storage and re-source development. Seminole warriors owned saddles, horses and guns that they purchased from the Spanish. The Smithsonian Museum in Washington, D. C. will donate collections to the Seminoles once their museum has the room for them.

The fifth building will be devoted to a historical journey, from Prehistoric man to the European Invasion of the new world. Artifacts from Indian archeological sites will be an integral part of this historical odyssey.

Building number six is an exhibition hall which will explain how descendants from many tribes of the Creek Confederacy made their way to northern and central Florida in the early 1700's. The spirit of the Seminole will be evident in the sensitive treatment of their Native American culture and early communal life.

The vast Seminole rangeland is lush and green. Cattle graze in herds mixed with Jersey, Guernsey and Herefords. There are also Angus and Brahma cattle wandering contentedly over the fields. Plenty of ponds exist where the cows cool off in knee-deep water. They appeared to be stuck there, but then in another pasture three more were taking advantage of this bovine form of air-conditioning.

The Everglades permeates your consciousness. At the campgrounds, there are signs of human intrusion. The Seminole police force patrol in their white cars with the official Seminole police seal painted on the door. An RV from California is parked in one of the choice spots in the shade. The park managers, a man and wife, keep a friendly eye on visitors. Riding over in a golf cart, they check in a guest for the night.

The RV park contains five one-room cabins and numerous RV hookups. Summer is off-season for Big Cypress park and there are no scheduled activities being held in the dining room. The cabins are very basic with a refrigerator and microwave.

The airstrip where Chief James Billie keeps his plane is just across the entryway to the park. The chief loves to fly. Once he took his friend Robb Tiller to the rattlesnake roundup in Texas to buy snakes for the reservation.

Pat Diamond accompanied them. Pat is Chief Billie's secretary. They all ended up in Texas where cowboys had spent weeks rounding up 200 to 300 live rattlers. They had planned to just go up to Tallahassee overnight. Instead, they ended up staying away for eight days.

Billie took off his shoes and stepped into a pen with at least two hundred live rattlers. Because he knew how to walk among them, the chief wasn't touched.

"That's that Indian from Florida that we've heard about," said one of the spectators at the snake roundup.

Negotiations were conducted for purchasing the snakes. "You mean you're going to take them home alive?" asked the incredulous snake dealer. "No one does that."

No one, of course, except Chief James Billie. He gave Pat $100 to buy some pillowcases. They had not brought cages with them for the snakes. He plunked the rattlers into the pillowcases, then swirled them around to get them dizzy and closed the cases.

The venomous rattlesnakes were boarded onto the floor of the plane, much to Pat's chagrin, who had to sit in the back of the plane with her feet up to avoid stepping on the rattlers all the way back home.

When James was doing some alligator wrestling down in Hollywood, there were more than a proportionate share of good looking women in the audience. He flexed his muscles so that they'd be impressed and get a good look at him. One woman in the audience had on a short skirt and James noticed that she wasn't wearing any underwear. "I removed my attention from the pit to get a better look at her and a hungry alligator almost bit off my thumb!"

The alligator wrestlers at Billie Swamp Safari have

183

sustained their share of finger injuries too. "Yeah, we've had some real bad luck with those guys," Billie said. There is still a dirt road going out to the compound. Not too many of the employees can drive an airboat. The museum is under construction. Yet a sense of purpose pervades the air.

Ian Tyson was the alligator wrestler. He and Daniel Yzaguirre had large poles that they used to poke the alligators and crocodiles in the pen, which was a pool of water surrounded by a sandy shore.

The gator that was going to be wrestled was a feisty one. About 10 years old, he started hissing when they poked him with the pole. His mouth looked cavernous. His teeth glistened in the sunlight.

I asked the German boy next to me if he was going to jump in with them, but he didn't understand English.

Ian, dressed in a Seminole shirt, jeans and barefoot, was a husky young man with curly hair and blue eyes. He started the show by passing his hand through the space between the alligator's open jaws. Then the gator snapped them shut. It was exciting to watch.

Swamp Owl said they were tiring the alligator out, but he looked ready for a fight to the crowd of spectators. There was also a crocodile in the pit which opened his mouth ready for a meal, but Daniel Yzaguirre kept him in check with his pole.

The alligator, about 10 feet long, has already got one wrestler's thumb in his stomach. Ian poked his pole and the gator went into a spin. Then Ian jumped on his back. He pulled open his jaws. Then Swamp Owl explained how the gators have three eyelids and tiny flaps over their ears. They have a flap in their mouth which was visible when he hissed and also when Ian opened his jaws.

The alligator was not afraid of the crowd. Ian took a piece of rope and tied up the gator's jaws. Then he untied the rope and held the alligator's snout with just the tip of his chin. An alligator has a very weak muscle opening his jaw but a steel-like snap when he closes it. A wrestler was too slow passing his hand through those jaws during one of the shows so this gator snapped down on his hand. Swamp had to put his fingers in the gator's ears to get him to open his jaws to extract his hand.

Ian passed his hand between those gaping jaws again. In the wild, the gator opens his mouth and waits for a bird to light there. It was scary to watch his split-second timing. Luckily, Ian wasn't hurt during this maneuver.

There are always businessmen showing up at the Safari who want to sell Chief Billie their products. On one occasion, a salesman for a cellular phone territory showed up.

"Where is the chief?" he asked James.

"He's around here somewhere," answered Chief Billie.

"Well I've got a product that I know he'll be interested in," said the salesman. "This will be a great investment for him. I can't wait to tell him all about it. By the way, what did you say your name was?"

"I'm Jim," said James.

James was enjoying pretending he was someone else. When he finally caught on, the salesman convinced the chief that GTE was a good investment. They bought a license for $30,000 and have made money with it.

That same salesman went with James to meet Attorney Jim Shore. They needed to discuss some legal details of the transaction. The salesman stuck out his hand to shake hands with Attorney Shore. No reaction. He did it again. Still the attorney didn't shake hands with him. He looked

185

at Chief Billie in a puzzled fashion.

"Do you see that white cane with a red top?"

"Yes."

"Do you know who carries that kind of cane?"

Slowly it dawned on the salesman that attorney Shore didn't shake his hand because he was blind.

Leslie's grandmother, Robb Tiller and
Craig Talesman at roundup

Chapter 19

Future Theme Parks

There is a personal magnetism about James that influences everything he touches. He is concerned about providing a good role model to his Seminole boys. He gives advice to the young men who surround him at Billie Swamp Safari. They sometimes get bored on the reservation, which he can't understand.

James Billie is interested in developing projects in the theme park field. There are 700 different theme parks in the United States, so it stands to reason one on the Indian reservation would make financial sense to the Indians. Not only would it be fun, but their rich culture and fascinating heritage would be educational to children who want to learn about the Native Americans who roamed this land long before the white man landed.

There is a great deal of competition in this business. Busch Gardens obtained a panda bear to enhance its appeal and this addition brought up admissions enormously. Disney World has grown by creating hotels with Polynesian, wild west, international, and river themes. Epcot and Universal studios appeal to adults as well as children.

"There are some 300,000 school children that would attend, but the schools don't have any money," commented the chief on the subject of theme parks. "Here's a proposal I'm considering now." It would include a hotel, a water park, an animal exhibit and several cultural exhibits.

Dr. James Fatigan has spent much of his life "hopping around at the top level of businesses." He has met many unusual people. As a psychologist, he helped found the Institute of Noetic Science in Palo Alto, California. He was a partner of Ed Mitchell, the astronaut, doing work in Washington in the area of organizational development.

"I heard a lot of opinions about Chief Billie before I met him. I had some biases, I'll have to admit. I had a great deal of curiosity about him. I thought he'd be egocentric, caught up in his own backwash. Many people lose their perspective. I spent three days with him and was knocked directly off my feet. The way people process information tells a lot about them. I had no idea he had the grasp of things he did.

"I underestimated him in two ways: first, he's not egocentric and, second, he's extremely intelligent. As I looked at his brightness, I could understand how he would maintain his wisdom because he has an incredibly firm value system.

"I have always made the first cut in life between talkers and doers. All the moguls and greats in our society were doers. They did it their own way. He is a leader of leaders.

"My specialty is in neuroscience. The right side of the brain controls visual and conceptual information and the left side controls verbal information. Chief Billie uses a balance of the two.

"Have you noticed his timing? He knows when to enter and when to leave. He does it so well you're not aware of it. When I'm around some important people they make you aware how you're taking up their time. He's not like that. When he enters and leaves, it's well-balanced. He gets what he wants accomplished. It's like he's listening with a third ear."

A musician he plays with named Jay Roberts said, "He has his own meter. I've met other musicians who have that. I can follow him, but it's his own sound."

Put another way, Dr. Fatigan said, "You know the computer language DOS? It's like he has his own DOS. What a unique combination of things. I don't think I've ever met that combination of things before. He's good at music and how he orchestrates.

"I sit in awe. This happens to be one of the most balanced intellectuals outside of a formal education. He's deeply curious about religion. I had a two hour conversation with him. He's part Irish, like me. The white man's world is full of defects. We're running off at one direction at a high speed. The Indians have maintained the balance to some extent. The way organized religion puts things together is full of irregularities.

"I am a street kid from New Jersey. When I was at Florida State in Tallahassee on a gymnastic scholarship, I almost quit and joined the seminary. I asked the question 'What's life about?'

"In the 50's I was doing work on intelligence tests. One of the factors the intelligence tests measure is how a person processes information. Chief Billie's way is totally fascinating. He is very quick. He told me, 'God never spoke to me. If there is a God, strike me dead. Better yet, use Robb.'"

189

Not only is it fascinating, but his genius is multi-dimensional. There are many people in a generation who are experts in one particular area. Einstein was a genius at physics, but not at human relations. Leonard Bernstein was a major musical talent. Winston Churchill was an outstanding diplomat and writer. John Kennedy had charisma, but made political blunders.

"Chief Billie is masterful at every game he plays. He performs equally well at music, hunting, politics, fighting, construction, economic development and law enforcement. He can run heavy equipment, fly a plane and helicopter, captain a yacht, drive a bulldozer or tank, brand cattle and wrestle alligators with ease. He is a perfectionist who changes his mind all the time. His projects are approached with vision and caution. His lack of fear makes him a calculated risktaker.

"I make sure I win," he says.

James is always giving advice. He is compassionate and tough at the same time. He gets the best from people because he is always giving his best. Whether driving a powerful airboat, or singing a romantic song, the Seminole chief is always thinking and planning his next course of action. He took us on his airboat for a ride.

"Look for a little red flower," said James as we sped through the swamp grasses and small trees. Sure enough, a few tiny spots of red emerged among all the sawgrass and thick palm forests. An animal had died inside a hummock because a buzzard was circling overhead and there was a rotten stench in the air. James jumped out with his boots and long pants on to investigate.

"We had a male antelope that had scratches on his rear where a panther had gotten him," explained James.

190

"He's probably the dead animal. I haven't seen him around lately."

We came suddenly upon a large buck whose antlers were the exact color of the grey tree branches around us. The noise of the airboat scared him into the dense woods. His white tail was the last trace of him as he bounded away.

Chief Billie and author aboard his airboat.

James pointed to a spit of land where he is building an alligator pit for his video. A large pile of sand stood in the middle of the canal. Next to it was a wire pen where the 14 foot alligator is presently housed.

Inside some boxes, rattlesnakes were peeking through the cracks and shaking their tails angrily. A new snake house is presently under construction.

191

One of the young Seminoles had recently been beaten by someone who was trying to get him to drink beer. His nose was scratched and swollen, but otherwise, only his pride was hurt. Chief Billie questioned him about the fight.

Dr. Fatigan is now in the entertainment business. He ran a show at Epcot Circus for Disney World in Orlando. He envisions an educational theme park somewhere in South Florida. He has also brought a proposal for "Gatorland" to James. So far the theme park idea is in the planning stages, but Chief Billie is exploring his options.

Architect John Randal McDonald is designing plans for a 1600 acre theme park. This projected authentic Native American theme park will demonstrate the cultures and customs of all the tribes in one place. Orlando has been proposed because there are many tourists who go there for vacations. This project will be along the lines of the Polynesian Cultural Center on the North shore of Oahu in Hawaii, but will include a casino in the complex.

James has been interested in the idea of a Seminole Indian Cultural Center for a long time. A model of this project was built at a cost of $2,200 when the building was slated to be built on land along Route 27 in Moore Haven. This center was going to be financed by the federal government, but those funds didn't come through.

Chief Billie is discussing many future projects with developers who would like to bring his visions to life. When his plans come to fruition, Indian theme parks will be lasting memorials to the culture of Native Americans presented in palatable and entertaining formats.

Influencing Other Tribes

Chief Billie has consistently encouraged other tribes to venture into Bingo and resorts. He has entered into joint ventures with them to foster economic development for his people.

The Seminole Tribe of Oklahoma is closely allied with the Seminole Tribe of Florida. The 12,000 member Seminole Tribe of Oklahoma under the leadership of Chief Jerry Haney has just announced plans to open Sweetwater Family Resort, a project which has support from U.S. Representative Pete Peterson, a Democrat from Marianna and Jim Fields, a superintendent with the U.S. Bureau of Indian Affairs. About 60 miles west of Tallahassee, the Florida panhandle supports this project as a way to create jobs.

The Oklahoma Seminoles were recently awarded $53 million from the United States Government for land taken from the Indians in 1832. Plans include a 1,700 acre site which would feature a bingo hall for 3,000 people, a hotel, shopping mall, convention center, water park, and cultural heritage museum. The current plan doesn't include a casino, but that possibility will not be ruled out for the future.

"This isn't a casino in disguise," Michael Haney, brother of Chief Jerry Haney announced at a news conference. "This is a coming home for the Seminole Nation that we've been looking for years and years."

The development has been discussed with Chief James Billie, who has given it a thumbs up. The resort is slated to cost an estimated $150 to $200 million to complete over a two-year period. Financing would be through tax-exempt revenue bonds issued by the Seminoles and backed by revenue generated by the attractions, officials said.

Haney said the Seminole Nation had no plans to expand their gaming beyond bingo. He wants to see how the casino referendums fare before Florida voters before taking any position on casinos.

"We're a very patient people. We waited 160 years to correct an injustice," he said. "We're willing to let the gaming things run their course."

There would be no danger of competition from the 5 existing Seminole Bingo Halls because of the distance from all of them. It is to Chief Billie's credit that he has set the standard for bingo all over the country.

Future ventures will capitalize on the successes the Native American tribes have achieved with this unique endeavor. It is important to realize that without James' determination and foresight, the dreams many tribes have realized today would have been mere wishes and not realities. They would not have taken concrete shape, but be mere ghosts of thoughts escaping the dreamcatchers of Seminole tribal members.

Chapter 20

From Termination to Gaming

C hief Billie has a knack for attracting talented people from every race and walk of life to do his bidding. The challenge of getting all the diverse operations up and running demands his constant vigilance. His objective is to make money for the Seminoles. With gaming, he has found a clear shot to the stratosphere of empire builders. Although there is more government regulation than there was in the days of the robber barons, the opportunities for the Seminoles are unlimited.

President Eisenhower issued an Executive Order in 1953 to terminate 10 Indian tribes. These tribes owned large land holdings of pasture and timber land and the government was in favor of acquiring them. Twenty-five more tribes were listed for termination during Ike's administration.

"Frank Billie went to Congress in April of 1957 and told them not to terminate us," explained Joel Frank, Washington representative of the Indian Gaming Commission for the Seminoles. Frank Billie is James Billie's uncle.

The Seminoles' government agent was bound and determined to save the tribe from extinction. Virgil Harrington helped the Seminole Indians organize their tribal government.

Congress only removed that order in 1992. Until then, the law remained on the Congressional records. The present day Seminole Tribe of Florida (there is also a Seminole Tribe of Oklahoma) is composed of two governing bodies. The Tribal Council has as its chairman the chief of the tribe, currently James Billie. The constitution initially stipulated a five member council.

The president of the Seminole Tribe of Florida, Inc., Fred Smith, is vice chairman of the Seminole Tribal Council. This corporation has a Board of Directors. The chairman of the Tribal Council, James Billie, is vice president of the Seminole Tribe of Florida, Inc.

This corporation governs some, but not all, of the financial enterprises of the Seminole tribe. Negotiations can only be binding for up to 10 years.

Gaming must be approved by the Seminole Tribal Council. There are three categories of gaming: 1–traditional gambling and social games that are not conducted on a commercial basis, 2–bingo, pool, tip jars, card games that are not house banking games under the exclusive control of the tribe, and 3–all other forms of gambling such parimutuels, casinos and blackjack.

There are presently only two states in the country that do not allow gambling: Hawaii and Utah.

Oneida, New York has just gotten a new casino which Joel Frank feels, "will do well. New York doesn't allow slot machines so there are no slot machines. There are all kinds of table games there."

In October, 1988, Congress passed the National Indian Gaming Regulatory Act to control the business. "Many states allowed churches and clubs to hold Las Vegas night and bingo as fundraisers," explained the commissioner of gaming.

When a state and tribe reach an agreement, or compact, who would have jurisdiction is up for discussion. The federal government has no involvement until the state and tribes hash it out.

For a tribe to be successful in gaming, it must have access to millions of people. For example, the Pequots of Connecticut bus customers in from nearby Mystic and from neighboring New York to feed their restaurant and casino.

"States like Oklahoma would have to work harder at it because they have 30 or 40 different Indian tribes there," observes Joel Frank.

The demographics for the state of Florida are very favorable. It is the number one tourist destination in the United States. Ninety percent of the population lives on Florida's two coasts. Therefore, central Florida is accessible to most of the residents for day trips. Tourists either come to the many theme parks and natural attractions, such as the boating and fishing or come to leave on cruise ships for the outer islands.

With a budget in excess of $57 million, the Seminoles are a powerful force in economic development.

"Unless you think big, you don't get big," says Robb Tiller, one of the players in the bingo phenomenon. It is exactly this type of thinking that has stood the tribe in good stead in the last decade.

The success that has been enjoyed by the Pequots can

certainly be attained in central Florida, where a huge population of retired people with time and money presents an untapped market for casino gaming. The attractions of appetizing food, gator wresting by an Indian, airboat rides and casino nightlife are unique and unbeatable.

Inaccessibility, which has been both a savior and a curse for the Seminoles, is not going to be a problem when the word gets out what is planned for Big Cypress reservation. A 150 room hotel built connecting the present Bingo Hall will be a strong enticement to visit this future Seminole resort.

Kissimmee Billie, who was nearly captured by U.S. soldiers during the Seminole wars until she retreated to the Everglades, would not believe the changes in her domain. Fenced cattle pastures now cover the terrain where alligators roamed with wild boar, wild turkeys, deer, wolf, panthers and bear.

The magic of the surroundings instills a spiritual peace in the visitor, miles from the traffic of civilization. Out in the glades, the changes are slow in keeping with the natural rhythms of the seasons.

As one of the little Indian boys said when asked about the big alligator in the canal where he and his friends were launching their canoe, "We don't think about it." They proceeded to flip the canoe over, getting soaking wet and laughing with joy like children around the world.

At the annual Green Corn Dance where Indian boys are given their Miccosukee names, Jim Shore's name is "Sha-ka-dig-lud-ka" meaning "he who runs and falls." He was brought up on the Brighton Reservation. Son of a shaman, Jim Shore is general counsel and financial officer for the Seminole Tribe of Florida, Inc., a multi-million dollar corporation that invests in many types of business ventures.

"He's the closest man to the chief right now," pointed out Jack Skelding, attorney and Tallahassee lobbyist for the Seminoles. "He graduated from Stetson law school."

Jim Shore is a hardliner. He believes the government is his enemy. In an article titled "Legal Warrior" in *Florida Magazine* in March, 1993, Shore is quoted as follows:

"The mentality of the government hasn't changed in 200 years," Shore says. "As long as the Indian man is on the reservation and not making any problem, and as long as he is poor and in an impoverished situation, then the government can go through the motions of trying to save the humble red man. As long as he's selling his trinkets by the railroad track, then everything is well.

"But the minute that this Indian man tries to do things to try and better himself and his situation, right away the mainstream society, the government, whatever that is, will try to knock these props out from under him."

Jim Shore has had a long personal struggle. He was part of the Seminole road crew along with others from Brighton reservation. He lived with his family there. An athletic basketball player at 25, he was driving back from Moore Haven to Brighton Reservation. He had gone into town to play, but was driving home because the basketball game had been cancelled.

The car accident was to change his life forever. He doesn't remember exactly how it happened. Already blind in one eye, Shore's Buick was clipped by the oncoming vehicle on the two lane road 721. Shore was driving too fast and possibly his vehicle crossed the yellow line. Whatever the circumstances, his vehicle landed down the embankment and rested on a concrete drainage platform.

The accident left him permanently blind. Doctors tried to save his left eye, but several operations failed. Shore was going to have to spend the rest of his life without his sight.

He made a decision. Starting at North Florida Junior College in Madison, Jim went on to Stetson University in Deland. In 1980, after majoring in history, he went on to graduate from law school and pass the bar exam at 35. He was the first Seminole Indian to earn a law degree.

Chief Billie had just started his leadership of the Seminole tribe and so the timing was perfect. He hired Jim in November, 1980, and they have been a team ever since. There was no one better to represent the tribe than a Seminole who knew the white man's laws.

Jim's office staff reads briefs to him when outside lawyers prepare documents on the casino case now brewing. As reported in *The Seminole Tribune* of July 16, 1993, Shore described the gaming issue as "an ongoing thing that changes every month, every week." The issue of electronic gaming devices, now at the forefront of the controversy, remains unresolved. Since the chief is so concerned about being a good role model, he inspires the best out of those associated with him. Representation by Attorney Jim Shore has catapulted the Seminole Tribe into a solid economic position.

In a commentary about bingo, Jim Shore said, "Our games have not hurt charity bingo attendance. We don't attract the fraternalist or church player. Our players are a different kind of crowd. It's an entertainment experience, like going to Disney World."

The fact that the Seminoles are smart enough to have the son of a medicine man fight for them in the courtroom demonstrates the perseverance inherent in their mind-set. Even though they are outnumbered, the tribe gives the impression that they will always be a formidable adversary.

Many other attorneys are hired by the Seminole Tribe, but James' most trusted person is the one whose heart belongs to the Indians because he knows how they think and feel. Jim Shore is their legal warrior.

The first Florida Seminole reservation to have high stakes bingo was permitted by the Supreme Court decision Butterworth vs. Seminole Tribe of Florida. Hollywood was the site of the first bingo hall, which was built in 1979. Chief James Billie was the one who pursued this venture.

Bingo rapidly became a lucrative enterprise for Indian reservations throughout the country. Word spread like wildfire that state regulation had been banned by the Supreme Court. Any state allowing bingo games must allow Indian tribes to run the same games without limits.

In 1981, a second bingo hall was opened on the Tampa Seminole reservation. This operation became so popular that it was expanded in 1991 to include a 24-hour bingo palace.

A 92,000 square foot bingo hall was built on the Big Cypress reservation in 1987. Adding to the tribal coffers, the Brighton reservation has a bingo hall that seats 200 in a former barn run by a licensed tribal member.

Joel Frank, whose Indian name, Ne-hi-fug-coo, means "Big man," states that the Johnson Act was passed in the 50's. This law prohibited the transporting of gambling devices across state lines.

"The state can opt out of it by passing its own law, but the federal law applies unless the state preempts it."

Washington representative for the Seminole tribe, Frank is extremely knowledgeable about all legislation pertaining to gaming. He is on the Federal Gaming Commission that regulates Indian gambling. Congress set up the structure whereby type three gaming, in other words, games backed by the house, would be regulated by the states.

Chief Billie, if all goes as planned, may again be leading the Seminoles in their newest venture. Casino gambling will be a natural extension of the bingo halls they already run.

Is this an Indian trait? Or did the wheeler-dealer skill in negotiation come from Chief Billie's Irish father? Whatever its origin, Chief Billie is a larger-than-life force to be reckoned with, for he will challenge the white man's laws to the limit. It is this refusal to give up that is so intriguing about the man. He is an Indian with a frontier mentality that is reminiscent of the very men who caused the Indians' demise.

Of course, anyone who can wrestle alligators has to be afforded a certain amount of respect. Growing up with dangerous reptiles perhaps molds a child like Billie to become a great leader of his people. His early entrepreneurship must have taught him something about the white man's capitalism, for he has beaten the white man in court again and again.

Florida is being difficult on the issue of casinos because Governor Chiles doesn't personally approve of gaming. He would do away with current gaming if he could.

"The only involvement of the Indian Gaming Regulatory Act of 1988 is to approve ordinances and approve the management company of a casino," stated Frank.

First, we should examine the history of the Indians in North America. At the time of Columbus' arrival in 1492, "There were approximately three hundred different tribes in North America speaking perhaps as many as five hundred different languages. The poetic richness of each language was a mirror to nature, reflecting the beauties and characteristics of a particular tribe's region, whether mountains or plains, cedar or sage, showers or snows, buffalo or deer.[1]"

In other words, the Native Americans were not from a single tribe or culture. They had distinctly unique customs and languages. Some were not very civilized. The horrific practice of scalping an enemy has caused many a white man to lose a good night's sleep or worse. They were crafty. They could seemingly hear animals walking in the glades and hammocks. They could hop from tree to tree and not leave footprints. They could travel silently at night.

Against all odds, they survived the onslaught of the Europeans, although they were lied to, killed, beaten and raped.

[1] *From p.12 "Indians" by Joanna Cohan Scherer, 1973, Crown Pub.*

Now that the Indians are slowly moving up, protective legislation at the federal level is being challenged as unconstitutional because it favors the tribes.

The Bureau of Indian Affairs has historically tried to keep tabs on all that the Seminole Indians needed help in doing. Sometimes the help hasn't been forthcoming, as in the case where they would not advance money for bingo halls. Current Eastern Area Director for the BIA is Bill D. Ott and Seminole Agency Superintendent is Leland Keel. Chairman Billie keeps them apprised of all that is happening in the tribal council meetings.

It remains to be seen whether the Seminoles will rival the Pequots of Connecticut. The Pequot casino makes in excess of a billion dollars a year. With James Billie at the helm, chances are the Seminoles will give the Pequots some fierce competition.

Chapter 21

The Five Seminole Reservations

BRIGHTON RESERVATION

*I*ndian Prairie was acquired in 1935 and became known as Brighton Reservation. Ten Seminole families farmed there when the land was purchased by the Resettlement Administration. Cattle, pigs and chickens were subsequently allocated to each family. Today it contains a recreational vehicle park open to the public. Land area is 35,805 acres.

The former catfish hatchery has been converted to a turtle farm. There is a great demand for turtle meat in Taiwan and Singapore. Bob Grant, who has a farm in Mississippi, is supervising the program.

"We can tell the males from the females by the length of their tail and the shape," explained Grant. "We raise 100% females because they grow five times faster than the males. There's a pound and a half one, and this one's almost two pounds." Grant can tell their weight just from looking at them, he's seen so many turtles.

"This is the greatest game in town," he said. "There is the room where we keep the big breeder turtles. They lay eggs three times a year. An incubation room hatches the eggs. Turtles can smell water, so we put a container of water in with them so that when they hatch we can find them. Before we did this, they would be buried in the sand."

Chief Billie's half-brother Charles Hires, who goes by Chuck Billie, was also working there that day.

"I do whatever needs to be done," he said. "James and I had the same mother but different fathers."

At the farm, there are long tanks where the turtles are swimming. They are sorted according to their size. Larger turtles are kept outside in holding ponds.

Brighton holds a rodeo every summer on the reservation. There are points given for every event. The prize for the most points was a horse trailer. There are also cash awards. Cowboys go on a circuit, riding and roping to collect the most points for the year at rodeos throughout Florida.

"In the Glades, there are only three things you can do with a cow. You can ride it, you can rope it and you can breed it," said one cowgirl.

Competition is fierce among the bronco riders to gain the most points for the season. Rodeos are very popular events in Glades County, where the Brighton reservation is located. Lakeport is the closest town to the reservation.

Brighton, like all the five reservations, has several smoke shops, some arts and crafts stores and a bingo hall. There is also a Baptist church on the reservation. The Cattleman's Association has a grange hall where meetings are held.

Pastures with herds of cattle are the most common sight at Brighton. Lykes Brothers owns acres and acres of cattle pastures interspersed with the Indian-owned land.

HOLLYWOOD RESERVATION

The Seminole Tribe of Florida's administrative offices are located at 6073 Stirling Road, Hollywood, Florida. The reservation nearby houses the offices for *The Seminole Tribune,* the Seminole police station, several tobacco shops, the housing office and several other shops.

The Hollywood Reservation also consists of a subdivision of homes that, except for the chickens and chickees in the yards, looks like any other South Florida community.

A big event every year is the Seminole Fair, a four-day rodeo and dance festival that the Seminole Tribe of Florida sponsors. The rodeo takes place in Laura Mae Osceola stadium. Dancers, wild life shows, alligator wresting and singing round out the many activities.

There is a display of crafts, complete with blue, red, and white ribbons for first, second, and third prizes on view in the arts center. Seminole paintings, beadwork, clothing, patchwork, wood carving, dolls, and quilts are exhibited in a 4-H type manner.

Other Indian tribes are also invited to participate. A Navajo booth offered lovely silver jewelry and Indian crafts.

There is a Miss Seminole contest and a Junior Miss Seminole who are chosen at the fair.

The Florida Turnpike was constructed right through the reservation land. Chief Billie ordered the state to put up a sign saying that drivers are entering the Seminole Indian Reservation. Just rated AA, the turnpike is a big revenue producer for the state. What if the Seminole tribe decided to put its own toll booth on the road?

Hollywood Reservation has a large bingo hall on Route 441, with prizes up to $60,000. The expanded facility has new slot machines and an addition with card tables has been completed.

Over $170 million dollars in cash has been won at Hollywood bingo. The matinee session is held daily at noon and 2:30 p.m. The main evening session starts nightly at 7:15 p.m. and the night-owl bingo begins at 10:45 p.m. The bingo hall is the world's most famous and has been number one ten years in a row. Tax free cigarettes are sold and there are two large snack bars for refreshments. They offer valet parking.

Lightning Bingo, a new instant game, is the latest rage. From the high attendance, the game of bingo seems to be gaining popularity daily. An airplane buzzes by with a banner welcoming the tourists and regulars alike to the impelling Hollywood gaming tables.

There is also a tribal museum on 441 and several craft shops including the Anhinga Gallery run by Joe Dan Osceola. Several smoke shops are scattered along the road. These are owned and operated by individual tribal members. Native Village is across the street from the bingo hall where alligator wrestling is held.

The Hollywood reservation is not a farming community like Brighton, Big Cypress and Immokalee reservations.

IMMOKALEE RESERVATION

In December of 1979, the village of Immokalee became a federally recognized reservation. All Florida Seminole people are citizens of the United States. With the exception of hunting and fishing, Native Americans are subject to the civil and criminal jurisdiction of the State of Florida.

The Immokalee Bingo Hall is called "The Seminole Gaming Palace." Glitzer though smaller that the Hollywood Bingo Hall, the Immokalee reservation's gaming facility is managed by Jim Claire and employs many tribal members.

Glass doors topped by neon lights announce the restaurant, the "Palace Grill," the "Poker" card tables, and the "Bingo" room. There are slot machines with all kinds of games to play. A Las Vegas style operation, the Seminoles keep it filled by busing patrons in from Ft. Myers, 25 miles away.

In the middle, the Immokalee Seminole Gaming Palace has a full service bar. The payoffs seem to be good at the slot machines: my husband won $64. A daily bingo jackpot of several thousand dollars lures the aficionados of this game.

The town of Immokalee is mostly populated with Mexicans involved in the produce business. There is a small airport, several fruit packing plants, and other small businesses. Signs in one section of town are posted in Spanish.

209

TAMPA RESERVATION

Tampa is located on the site of an ancient Indian burial ground. When the town was excavating the site, bones were uncovered. The Seminoles rightfully claimed the land as their own. A native village was erected.

Several people are involved with the bingo hall that was built on the site. Bobby Henry, a shaman known as the "Rainmaker," Clarence Motlow and Jim Claire keep the day to day operations running smoothly. The parking lot is full of busses that bring players daily to play and win high stakes games. Slot machines have been added to the facility.

Alongside the bingo hall housing is available for the Seminole reservation Indians. Chickees in the yards attest to their presence.

There used to be a six-lane drive through smoke shop which the tribe operated. Tobacco is purchased in Georgia and the cigarettes are wholesaled to the Seminoles.

When the Seminoles acquired the reservation, Chief Billie told them he was going to use the land for "economic development." He intended to build a prosperous bingo hall there all along, but had he told the city specifically his intent, it would have been harder for him to acquire the necessary permission to develop the site.

He owns the Sheraton Inn which abuts the bingo hall. Mitchell Cypress, a tribal board member, manages the hotel for the chief. Known in Indian circles as "the playboy of the Everglades," Mitchell has been a friend of James's since they were boys.

They used to fight together in the schoolyard. Mitchell remembers James coming to church on Sunday once with his face all swelled up. He had gotten into a beehive and had welts all over.

BIG CYPRESS RESERVATION

Big Cypress reservation came from an original land purchase by Seminole agent Jacob E. Brecht, M.D. In 1909, he purchased land for the Seminoles which today forms the core of Indian-owned land in Florida. Swampy in places, the wide expanses of pasture make cattle ranching popular on Big Cypress and Brighton reservations.

Chief Billie lives on Big Cypress reservation with Leslie Garcia and their son, Micco. Since they own a herd of cattle, they recently had a calf named "Moo-Moo" in their yard. Micco owns two ponies named Macaroni and Peanut Butter.

Big Cypress is the reservation that has Billie Swamp Safari on it. There are citrus groves, vegetable farms and cattle everywhere.

The airstrip always contains an assortment of airplanes and helicopters. Some belong to visitors, but most are owned by the Seminole Tribe. James loves to fly and does so at every opportunity.

Big Cypress hosts a rodeo every year at its rodeo grounds. There is a modern row of stables where the rider's mounts are kept. Musicians and dancers entertain the crowds. Alligator wrestling is part of the show, as is a comedian and a band contest. Seminole pumpkin fry bread is available along with a tasty selection of Indian food. Like the other reservations, there are smoke shops and Indian craft stores for tourists. Ahfachkee Elementary School and a gymnasium help the youngsters develop their minds and bodies.

A festival named "Chalo Nitka," Miccosukee for "Big Bass," is held in the town of Moore Haven every year. Seminoles present a colorful program at the 3-day event which was started 43 years ago as a celebration for the completed paving of the town's Main Street. The Seminoles elect an Indian princess and hold contests to give prizes for the best Indian patchwork clothing. Their special food and handicrafts are sold at the many booths on the Chalo Nitka fairgrounds. A rodeo is part of this celebration held every March.

Chapter 22

A Typical Day

C hief Billie's day begins "when I get up." His Mexican maid cooks breakfast for the chief, Leslie, Micco, and any guests who stop in to see them. The kitchen is a hub where all the tribal members, employees, and guests congregate. The phone is always ringing and it is usually for James. The daily roster of business is dealt with in a quick call to Pat Diamond, his secretary at the tribal offices. There are several other callers who need to speak with the chief.

On this Friday, he was going to look at a crop dusting business. Ernest Hillard, the owner, lives in Moore Haven, a town about 45 minutes from the Big Cypress reservation. He is a farmer who has spent much of his life in this town. He owns two planes and several accounts. The price of the business was $450,000.

Robb Tiller, who lives on his river boat on Lake Okeechobee moored at the Thousand Adventures Marina, was ready to wheel and deal. Robb, my husband Thom, and I, drove over to the Hillard's place where the planes, a yellow Pratt and Whitney and another similar one were parked out on the grass. Robb warned us about the rottweiler chained behind the house to protect against prowlers.

"There they are," said Robb, as the Bell Jet Ranger helicopter came into view. "Let's show them where to land."

"They can see the runway," said Hillard. The morning was sunny. Only a slight breeze rustled over the verdant pasture.

There in the sky appeared the helicopter, getting larger and larger as it barreled towards land, a beige and white craft that skimmed over the citrus trees like a giant mosquito.

Chief Billie was navigating. Pilot Charles Kirkpatrick, 55, is a licensed airplane and helicopter instructor. He was in the C.I.A. and has logged more than 15,000 hours flying time in the 32 years he has been flying.

"I used to be afraid of helicopters because I had a few accidents. Then I had someone I was working for who wanted one, so I spent three hours a day studying and got my helicopter license in 10 days," Kirkpatrick said in a soft drawl. He walked around to the side to explain the fuel tank.

"Here are the switches for the two automatic fuel pumps. There is also one built into the system. This tank can be filled to increase the fuel capacity to 97 gallons."

The four seat Bell Jet Ranger was purchased for $60,000 from the telephone company and refurbished is worth $200,000.

Hillard explains the operation of the crop dusters to the chief. The bright yellow planes sit in front of a large barn that contains an airboat and several tractors. Micco picks up some rocks to aim at the wooden post in front of the barn. He sticks close to his parents. Then, with typical Billie curiosity, he walks over to the nearest plane and reaches up to touch the wing. He can just reach it.

Chief Billie picks Micco up around his waist and slings him in the truck with him. We all drive over to the Moore Haven restaurant for breakfast. The chief, Micco and Hillard ride in Hillard's truck.

The eight of us take up a long table. A waitress wearing Indian beaded earrings writes down our orders. One of the policemen in the town, a black man, has been shot. Chief Billie remembers that he worked for him at one time on the reservation.

The chief orders buttermilk. Leslie relates how their maid threw some away because she thought it was regular milk that had turned sour. We all have big appetites.

The discussion turns to Popeye. "He was my hero as a boy," says James. "The Indian boys would beat up on me and I'd see him eating spinach and getting strong from it."

"He'd suck the spinach in from his pipe," added Hillard.

One of the first buildings that went up on Big Cypress reservation was a gymnasium so that young men and women could keep their bodies in shape. Physical fitness has always been a priority with the chief.

"We're going to look at turtles," announced James after breakfast. Back at Hillard's farm. Chief Billie, Leslie, Micco, Charles, and I climb into the Bell Jet Ranger and head towards the Brighton reservation. We fly over miles and miles of swampy Everglades and pasture lands. The landscape is unmarred by houses, electrical wires or smokestacks. Cabbage palm hammocks and cypress trees create wooded areas amid the vast "river of grass" that forms fertile streams beneath us. Feed for fish and wildlife is abundant here.

Chief Billie circles the former catfish hatchery where the turtles swim. Leslie doesn't like flying over the areas of watery swamp in the helicopter, although she is taking lessons to learn to fly the two-seater. We land on a small spit of land between the natural pond where a turtle lifts his head above the glistening surface to eye us and the symmetrical tanks laid out precisely between the rows of grass. In these former catfish tanks, soft shell turtles will be raised for export.

I am instructed to run towards the front of the helicopter when exiting, because the tail rotor blade can swivel from side to side while stabilizing the craft. The most difficult part of helicopter piloting is hovering, according to Charles Kirkpatrick, a helicopter instructor.

We go into the manufactured home of Bob Grant, the supervisor for the project. He informs us that there are some people from Singapore who have just left. They are buyers for the turtle meat, which is supposed to be an aphrodisiac and therefore is prized in Asian countries. He hands the chief one can of turtle meat and one of salsa.

Turtle farming is a relatively recent Seminole business. Like much of the Everglades wildlife, soft shell turtles are becoming scarce. Ventures that raise them domestically can be successful if there is an international marketing program carried out to sell the meat.

One building is kept for the large breeder turtles, which lay eggs three times a year—about 60 per turtle. The farm consists of two structures. The breeder turtles are housed in a small outbuilding by themselves. The incubator is a large newer structure full of turtle eggs in sand and wooden shelves.

Fledgling baby turtles are kept in tanks according to

size. Their natural enemies are alligators. Burt Crowell, owner of Micco Boats, has seen one being devoured.

"I watched an alligator throw one up in the air and catch it, bearing down hard with his jaw. Alligators have weak muscles opening their mouths and strong ones closing them. Finally, the alligator pierced the soft shell. Since the turtle was large, the gator kept the turtle in its mouth until he could bite off a piece of the meat. I wish I had had a video camera because it was fascinating," Burt said.

Baby turtles are prey for water birds occasionally too. Safari workers have seen gators eat armadillos on their dune buggy tours around the Everglades. Buzzards clean up whatever happens to be killed by passing motorists on the roadways to and from the reservations.

The turtles are treated royally. Their water is kept clean and they are coddled and fed so that they will grow fast and put on weight rapidly.

A truck pulls up to the operation. Chuck Billie gets out, the chief's half-brother. The men sit around the kitchen table talking informally about the business. All of them are problem solvers, but the chief has the last word.

Then we pile back into the helicopter. The Bell Jet Ranger lifts up effortlessly then lunges forward at an angle. We cover the short distance to the grange in minutes. A helicopter is the most efficient form of transportation between Big Cypress and Brighton reservations. James mimics the way I run out of the helicopter. I bend, duck down my head, and run forward, although the blade is well out of reach. I'm not taking any chances. We have alighted smoothly on a soft grassy field like a giant eagle dropping out of the sky. Chief Billie's Indian name, "Hee-tum-tum," means "high" or "above" or "one who flies."

The freezing apparatus is housed in a building similar to a fish freezing plant. The turtles are kept cold overnight. Then they are brought out in burlap bags to be slaughtered. The process is not for the fainthearted. John White knows his trade.

He warns me away from the bucket where he will be throwing the entrails because I could be covered with blood. The turtles are expertly carved into sections, after being beheaded. There are large buckets where the pieces are sorted. He tosses them quickly as he works.

Then the meat is trimmed by another assistant butcher. She sorts the meat into pieces with fat and pieces without fat. It makes me curious about the taste of turtle meat because I have read a book *Survive the Savage Sea* where people were kept alive on turtle meat in the Pacific ocean.

Intent on watching the process, I fail to see James sneak up behind me. Mischievously, he presses the can of turtle meat against my bare leg. He gets the desired result when I yell with surprise. We fly back to the Big Cypress reservation where my husband is waiting. With him are Mr. and Mrs. Dave Hanlon from Resorts International.

Inside the Swamp Cafe, the turtle meat is spread out before us. I am anticipating a fishy taste, but much to my surprise and delight, it is very firm and tastes somewhat like venison. The chief talks about his plans for the future.

Then a fiddler, Jay Roberts, comes up and starts playing for us. It is a treat to hear live music at lunchtime from a professional fiddler. Chief Billie gets his guitar and joins in. They jam together for about two hours.

"He always has something new," observes Jay Roberts, who plays a very mean fiddle. "This one takes seven minutes."

The harmony is incredible in both their voices and their instruments. They are both obviously enjoying the session. People wander in and out of the Swamp Cafe all the while they are playing, but they are so intent on their music that it doesn't disturb them.

Now it is our turn to take a airboat ride. We spin around in the sawgrass a few times, then zoom off into the Everglades. I put on earplugs because the noise of the engine is deafening. The chief, as in everything he does, handles the airboat expertly.

The ride continues deeper into the wilds of the Seminole reservation. One would have to be an Indian to find his way in this dense place. Ahead we see some brush move. The buck's silver antlers are perfect camouflage in the palette of this wilderness. Our airboat scares him into flight. We see the twitch of his white tail disappear into the thicket.

Back at the auditorium, we sit chatting with the musicians, James and Jimmy McDaniels.

"I don't have any people here that have 2,000 hours," said the chief. That is the required experience in order to fly a crop duster.

James brings up the subject of the movie *The Last of the Mohegans.*

"My friends like Russell Means were going to be in the movie. We had a conversation that mostly consisted of insults. I'm not a criminal and I don't have anything against the Florida people." He lay down in the grass looking up at the clear blue sky. He was totally relaxed now.

"We're going to be filming an alligator video over there." James gestured towards the alligator pit across the canal. "We need to get a yellow dog."

"Alligators bring meat back to their burrows," said Thom.

"I've never seen them do that," said James skeptically.

"Yes, they sometimes will do that," said Jimmy, a wildlife biologist. "There's been times you'll see a partially digested animal in their nests."

"I do whatever needs to be done," said Chuck Billie, a husky black-haired Seminole. He was born nine years after James.

"I felt bad that the family got broken up," said the chief. "My mother died and then my grandmother died, so we got split up." Even as a boy, James felt a great sense of responsibility for his half-brother, Chuck. Now they work together on the many businesses of the Seminoles

After viewing the turtle hatchery, James flew his helicopter with Leslie Garcia, Micco, and me in the back, to the grange building a short distance away. A large cement building next to the cattleman's grange meeting house, it is where the turtles are prepared for export.

"I remember seeing an Indian take a turtle and go like this with his knife and completely gut it," reminisced the chief. He made quick motions with his hands to demonstrate the procedure. "He was fast. It only took a minute."

John White can butcher 100 turtles a day. He is quick to separate the parts which are then processed by a woman who cuts the fat off some and leaves it on others. They are both pros at their trade.

There are giant freezers there where the turtle meat is stored. The Seminole Tribe has orders for 5 million pounds of turtle meat.

"The Indians use turtles to eat the dead bodies over in the Ganges River where they throw the dead. Unfortunately, the Indians are hungry so they're eating the turtles," explained James.

The turtle meat is considered a delicacy in Taiwan and Singapore. James ordered bowls for the turtle meat. We ate some with our hands. It has a meaty flavor that is very good, similar to lamb.

Although the turtle enterprise is in its infancy, the Seminoles have the resources and ingenuity to make this farm a profitable one. Since the turtles are quickly disappearing from the fresh water ponds in the Everglades, raising them domestically is one solution for the future.

Burt Crowell made a turtle soup once when he was camping, but a tornado blew it over before he had a chance to taste it. Perhaps someday he'll have a chance to make another batch.

Turtle eggs are edible either mixed with chicken eggs or can be used with frying batter, according to John White, the turtle butcher. When a large breeder turtle is found, the female is returned to the Everglades so it will reproduce turtles in the ponds. In this way, the wild turtle population will be replenished. James continues striving to preserve the Everglades so it can be enjoyed by both whites and Indians.

221

Chief Billie works on his airboat engine.

Chapter 23

Mother Earth

"There are no other Everglades in the world."
—*The Everglades River of Grass* by Marjorie Stoneman Douglas

C hief Billie is determined to use the Seminole's love
for the Everglades to foster economic development.
He has started a farming program on 500 acres
which will produce vegetables to be sold to local super-
markets. There is a natural respect for the rhythms of
nature that is imbued in the Native American soul.

The Seminoles' love affair with the Everglades has
lasted since they arrived on the fertile Florida soil. The
poetry of their songs and legends has been whispered in
the sawgrass and palmetto. They have shared stories
around their smoky campfires, protected runaway slaves
from savage owners and taught their children shaman
rituals and Indian customs.

"If I see something dying off, I just think it's meant to
be that way," explained James. "Every question about the
Everglades cleanup is still going to be a question when
they're done. They're just BandAid jobs. The folklore
calls the high terrain area north of the lake 'the land
where the earth is alive.' There the grounds have reddish
earth where there are minerals and where fruits and
apples grow.

223

"We believe that a big earthquake happens because nature meant it to be that way," James explained patiently.

"This has been a dream for me for twenty-three years," said Jimmy McDaniels, a Creek Indian from Tallahassee who worked for the Florida Game and Fish Commission for 31 years. He's known James for the past 20 years. Jimmy was their wildlife biologist for the Northwest Florida region.

"When do you want to retire?" James asked Jimmy about three years ago. "We're ready when you are," said the chief. Jimmy was the northwest alligator regional coordinator, head of the Nuisance Alligator Program. People would call in when an alligator had eaten their dog or threatened them. He had six people working for him.

"I came down here in 1970 when Joe Billie was co-chairman of the Governor's Council on Indian Affairs. I looked at Brighton and Big Cypress. Brighton is definitely a good area for quail hunting."

The chief talked a long time ago about creating wild hog hunting here on Big Cypress and quail hunting on Brighton reservation. Jimmy looked it over and said it was feasible. The chief was looking for something that could be done to make some money. Jimmy thinks that Chief Billie is one in a million—no, make that one in 10 million!

The Everglades still has the mercury problem. They are finding exotic fish such as Oscars that are following the flowing water into new areas. Exotic trees such as the melaleuca are now a concern. The U. S. Department of Agriculture imported them from Australia to dry up the

Everglades. They spread unchecked and now are considered by some to be a pest.

"When I was involved in a duck hunting program, we flooded the fields to attract the ducks. Not counting the cost of personnel, we figured it cost us about $30 per duck," said the wildlife biologist.

The beauty of these hunting programs is that they will improve the rest of the ecology of the Everglades. The hogs and deer will improve the habitat for the bears and panthers that live in this area already. They will have more prey and can easily get a better diet. Additional burning will also enhance their habitat.

Back in 1909, before they put canals through, this part of the Everglades used to be grass prairie. There was Brown's boat landing and the old schoolhouse. All that was water. The cattlemen needed grasslands for their cattle. Now the prairie has died out and been replaced with wax myrtle salt palmetto. It has all changed in the last 30 to 40 years.

"Our government has messed everything up," said Jimmy. "They put Alligator Alley through and it stopped the natural flow of the water. If they had put it up so it didn't interfere with the natural flow, the ecology would be preserved. But they didn't do it that way. Now there are bushes growing where there used to be sawgrass. Miami needs so much water. They made canals so Miami can use the Everglades water for their drinking water. Now they have all these road systems. The small farmers are just one part of the picture. It's not their fault that the problem exists. They didn't make the canals."

Jimmy met James Billie in 1975 in Tallahassee where he told him about his ideas. The chief thought it was a good opportunity. They were attending the Governor's council where members get acquainted with the legislature

"I asked him, 'When are you going to start this?' In the past four or five years he told me he was really serious. He asked when I was going to retire. I got fed up with all the bureaucracy. There was too much paperwork. I wanted to get back into the woods and swamps," Jimmy told the chief.

In August, 1991, James invited Jimmy to come on down and work for the tribe. After 23 years his dream came true. *Tallahassee Magazine* did an article on his retirement.

His mother was a Creek out of South Georgia so he considers himself a Florida Creek. He was raised on a hunting plantation. Jimmy had to excuse himself to check with a tour leader who was chaperoning a busload of German tourists visiting Billie Swamp Safari. Before he sat down to talk, Jimmy McDaniels was out driving the airboat, which had just come back from being repaired because it had been porpoising.

Fleishman owned 10,000 acres up in Tallahassee. He was a multimillionaire whose hobby was quail hunting. The birds were kept in their natural habitat. They used to burn the woods every year in late January to make the ideal quail habitat. The burning sets back the plant secession.

"The quail is a gallinaceous bird that eats insects and seeds. The annuals come back every year. Beggarweeds and legumes came after the fire. They start growing in March, so we created a perfect habitat for them," Jimmy said.

In Tallahassee, many black tenant farmers paid $10 a month to work the land. They farmed with a mule and didn't use insecticides or herbicides. This created an excellent habitat for the quail. If you kill off the weeds, the quail don't have any food.

There people would come out to hunt. There were 10 or 15 large plantations there then, each consisting of between 10,000 and 15,000 acres. They were used strictly for the owner's pleasure. There were the Baker family, the U.S. Steel owners, the Campbell's Soup heirs. They would bring out their guests. With 100 bird dogs and a mule-drawn wagon, the hunters were ready. A guy on horseback would flush out the quail. The groups of hunters would come and leave all year long. They figured it up and one bird would be worth about $15,000 for the expense of it all. They could kill three birds out of a covey.

The chief has already picked out the area in Brighton. There is an area of prairie. He'll buy the birds from a game farm. He has 1,500 acres. The hunters can use any type of shotgun. They considered pheasants, but those birds run more than they fly. It will cost $300 a day and they can shoot 10 to 12 birds. Additional birds will cost more.

The quail whistle to each other. The ones left behind will call to each other, so they can put one in a trap and all the others will come to that one and enter the trap. Next July we'll start the quail hunting program.

Since there are a lot of Spanish people in Miami, a wild hog program was introduced on Big Cypress. The weekend of October 23-24, 1993, was the Seminoles' first hunt. They have over 700 wild hogs on the reservation.

There were six hunters on Saturday and six hunters on Sunday. A flat charge of $250 includes a chickee for the night and three meals—dinner, breakfast, and lunch the next day, or hunters can pay $200 for a single day hunt. The hunters shoot with rifles. There is a $15 charge to skin the animals.

They also have a deer hunt. There are 100 axis deer from India. No license is required to hunt the wild hogs or axis deer. Non-tribal members need a license to hunt the doves or snipe here.

James has all these visions. He's determined to bring the tribe into the 21st century. He envisions a slaughter house where the deer meat can be processed and served here at the Swamp Water Cafe. If the deer meat is aged 30 days, it can be char-broiled with a strip of bacon around so it tastes like filet mignon.

Chief Billie and Jimmy McDaniels both like to cook. "My idea is a **swamp critter plate**," said Jimmy. "We could serve some alligator, frog legs, turtle meat, deer, duck, and quail. There are some crayfish that when it rains hard come up and cross the road. We could have some 'swamp bugs.' We wouldn't use those. We'd buy them."

"We all see Big Cypress as a big resort in the future except the Everglades where we want to provide camping tours with hunting and fishing and hiking," said Jimmy.

Birdwatchers would delight in the plentiful variety on the Big Cypress reservation. Woodpeckers, swallow-tail kites, bitterns, coots, wood storks, and egrets are common sights. Red hawks soared overhead. The tranquility is a welcome respite.

James is adamant about keeping the area clean and

unpolluted. He is a conservationist with a vast knowledge of the natural waterways feeding into the Big Cypress reservation. Bert Crowell, a bass fisherman also familiar with the Everglades ecology, said that there are just as many fish in the Everglades as ever because there is enough food for them. "The supply of fish is determined by the amount of food available to them."

The Seminoles have had a symbiotic relationship with the Everglades since they arrived in Florida and were nurtured in its protective bosom. The hunting of deer and bear has gone on for generations. The proud Seminoles have canoed silently along the rivers, fished the plentiful streams, hunted the white-tailed deer, and carved their dugout canoes and their chickee poles from cypress wood.

"We never thought the deer would be gone," said the chief.

John Anderson wrote the song *Seminole Wind* while visiting the Big Cypress reservation. The verses played on the loud speaker at lunchtime at the Swamp Water Cafe. There is a serenity on the reservation that renews the mind and refreshes the spirit. The unhurried pace mirrors the rhythm of the true Seminole—measured, precise and reverent. The miles and miles of woodlands, swamps and pasture where cattle roam give the visitor the meter of "Indian time." A lone coyote crosses the road in front of a car. The warm summer sun beats down on the lush emerald grasses. A quiet elegance descends, away from the noises and traffic of the coastal cities.

"We don't do anything in the summer because that's when the body needs to rest. The body only functions at a certain temperature. Something evil happens to you if you stay out in the sun too long," says James. "White people think that this is laziness, but it is just the Indian way."

Thom, Robb Tiller and Micco at roundup

Chapter 24

Taking Off With Aircraft

The Seminoles have explored many opportunities for investing the money they earn from bingo and gaming. One of the areas that has always been of personal interest to Chief Billie is aircraft. The Meyers 210 Spirit is an airplane model that hasn't been manufactured in 40 years, but aviation buffs remember the plane fondly. The Seminole Tribe is planning to bring back the airplane by manufacturing a new version based on the old design. The Meyers aircraft motto is "rekindle the spirit."

Engineer/inventor Milt Kimball is in charge of the project. Dan Hunsinger and his wife manned a booth at Sun 'n Fun in Lakeland, Florida, where an experimental version of the Meyers was displayed. The 20th annual Fly-in at Lakeland Linder Airport attracted 750,000 people from all over the country from April 10-16, 1994.

Pilots, kit plane enthusiasts, replica builders and classic restorers attended workshops in their field of interest. Movies with an aviation theme, such as the premiere of *Amelia Earhart*, a made-for-television movie starring Diane Keaton, were featured. An RV park housed pilots and participants staying the whole week.

"The manufacture of the Meyers is a great opportunity

231

for the Seminoles," said Dan with enthusiasm. "Let's face it, gambling is not going to last forever. This is a growing industry."

"We were flying into Hollywood to go to the reservation several years back. James said to me, 'I know this airport's here somewhere.' That was in the days before he had his pilot's license," said Skeets. James was notorious among pilots all over Florida because he logged on 600 hours before he was officially licensed. Every pilot from Tallahassee to Key West had heard about him.

"He always liked to push the law," said Skeets.

"Another time we were flying in from Marco Island. It was a full moon, but there was a ground fog, so James couldn't see the runway. It wasn't visible from the air." They were worried because they couldn't see the ground either.

"There's the bingo hall," Skeets pointed out to him finally after they had circled and circled.

"OK. Now watch for the white strip," said the chief.

The Seminole police came out onto the runway to shine their lights, but they were blinding James in the cockpit. Unfortunately, the white strip wasn't visible from the air and there were no landing lights on the field. Somehow James managed to land the plane.

The very next day, James ordered a strobe light for the water tower. Now the Big Cypress airstrip is the scene of fly-ins throughout the year. Future plans include expansion of the airport from the current 4,000 foot runway to a 7,000 foot asphalt airstrip to accommodate jets.

Big Cypress also holds motorcycle rallies called Ride-ins for Harley lovers. Miles and miles of back roads make Big Cypress a biker's paradise.

Jerry Cobb, a missionary in South America, was the pilot who certified James. A matter-of-fact person, she is as outspoken as James.

"The first time I met him I exclaimed, 'You're the most bowlegged man I've ever met.' He said I should have seen his legs before the operations he's had." Jerry Cobb likes the wide open spaces and is moving from the town of Moore Haven to a 100-acre farm.

"Don't blame me for his flying," she said. "I'm not responsible for that."

One day the chief was headed for New Orleans. Thunder and lightning appeared in the dark sky. He didn't know what to do, so he called Jerry from the air.

"James asked me what he should do. I said to him, 'James, just turn around quickly and come back'."

Jerry owns four labrador dogs who are all related and a beautiful collection of orchids. She lives in an old house on the Caloosahatchee River that will be turned into an antique shop.

Chief Billie's fertile mind and personal charm are paving the way for a strong Seminole future. The Seminole tribe's foray into airplanes is indicative of their willingness to explore many types of capitalistic enterprises.

They have already stirred up interest in the Meyers aircraft project from diverse foreign markets. James is willing to learn techniques for marketing their aircraft to countries on the Pacific rim.

The vice president of Thousand Adventures, Inc., Kenny Vopnford, was visiting Big Cypress reservation on a business trip. He had connections to make in Ft. Myers for his return trip to Nebraska.

"I'll fly you to the airport in time to make your flight," promised Chief James Billie. His plane was a 210 which carried six passengers. He kept it on the airstrip next to the campgrounds at the reservation. It was the site of fly-ins by pilots of small planes.

The night before they had attended a softball game in which the chief's daughter was on one of the teams. Although the team's performance was far from stellar, the chief made the players feel as if they had won the world series. He was proud to watch the young people succeed. After touring Billie Swamp Safari, Kenny and the chief drove to the airport.

They went to start the plane, but the battery was dead. Undaunted, the chief drove a giant crane onto the runway. He obtained a pair of jumper cables and raised Kenny up in the crane. The wind was fierce that day. Kenny was afraid he would be blown over as he was balancing with the hot wires on the airplane battery. Miraculously, the plane got started.

They taxied down the runway and lifted off into the ever darkening sky to the Northwest of them. They encountered air turbulence from the worsening weather. The sky was a furious mixture of wind and clouds.

Oblivious of the worsening conditions, the chief asked Kenny, "Have you ever flown before?"

"No, I haven't, Chief."

"Here are the controls. Try it." He handed over the piloting of the airplane to a complete novice.

"The weather is changing for the worse. I'm going down low. If you see any trees out your side let me know about them." The fog was now as thick as pea soup.

The lights were blinking on and off so the chief couldn't tell whether the landing gear had dropped. He went back to the manual control and pumped and pumped swiftly.

When James Billie was given an Indian name at the Green Corn Dance, his name was "Hee-tum-tum," meaning "high", or "above" or "he who flies." He thought back to this ceremony and got his second wind.

"Is your wheel down? Mine is on this side." Kenny looked out the window and could barely discern his wheel underneath through the blinding atmosphere of fog.

"I can't see. Wait. Yes, Chief, mine's ready." But unfortunately, they had no way of seeing under the nose. They would have to land without knowing whether the front wheel had been released because there was no way to ascertain it was down from inside the cockpit.

"There are three jets in back of us waiting to land. We can't circle around again. We have to land now. Well, I guess today is as good a day as any to die."

BIBLIOGRAPHY

Newspapers

The Seminole Tribune Various issues, mostly from the years 1986-1994

The Key West Inquirer

The Miami Herald "Tropic" Section *"The Great Indian Bingo War"* October 31, 1993

The New York Times "Some Indians See a Gamble with Future in Casinos" May 15, 1994

The Palm Beach Post August 31, 1993 article on Billie Swamp Safari

Ft. Lauderdale News January 14, 1984, January 10, 1985

The Sun-Sentinel March 15, 1987

The Sun-Tattler May 19, 1984 *"Seminole Indian Nation Chief James Billie: Preserving Yesterday, Planning for Tomorrow"*

The Seattle Times January 30 and April 30, 1985 Bingo articles

Tulsa World April 8, 1984 *"Playing for Keeps–World's Largest Bingo Hall Opens"*

Daily Globe News January 27, 1985 *"New Muckleshoot cry: BINGO"*

XS "Cashing in on Bingo; Are the Seminole Indians Married to the Mob?" February 16-22, 1994

Periodicals

Bingo Bugle 1993 & 1994 issues

Seminole American Indian Magazine official publication of the Seminole Tribe of Florida, Inc. Hollywood, FL, 1987

Time Magazine January 2, 1984 *"Indian War Cry: Bingo!"*

Forbes July 2, 1984 *"Filling the Bottom Line"*

Florida Magazine March 21, 1993 *"Legal Warrior"*

Florida Anthropologigt Vol. XI. No. 3 Boyd, Mark Frederick *"Horatio S. Dexter and events leading to the Treaty of Moultrie Creek with the Seminole Indians."* February, 1958

Florida Dept. of State "First Citizens and other Florida Folks" Tallahassee, FL, 1984

Florida Trend February, 1994 *"Blue Highway Eateries"*

Na-Ga-Tha-Thi-Ki "Something to Learn—Something to Remember" Seminole Tribe of Florida 1990

National Geographic "The Everglades; Dying for Help" April, 1994 and *"The Violent Saga of a Maya Kingdom"* February, 1993

Smithsonian August, 1993 *"Jaysho, moasi, dibeh, ayeshi, hasclish-nih, beshlo, shush, gini"*

Films

The Kingdom of the Maya, National Geographic, George Stuart, 1993

Books

Bemrose, John *Reminiscences of the Second Seminole War* University of Florida, Gainesville, FL, 1966

Bonnin, Gertrude (Zitkala-Sa) *American Indian Stories* Hayworth Publishing House, Washington, DC, 1921

Bradkin, Cheryl Greider *The Seminole Patchwork Book* 1978

Brandebourg, Margaret *Seminole Patchwork* Sterling Press, N.Y., 1987

Buker, George E. *Swamp Sailors: Riverine Warfare in the Ever-glades 1835-1842.* University Press of Florlda, Gainesville, FL, 1975

237

Bullen, Adelaide K. *Florida Indians of Past and Present* University of Florida, Gainesville, FL 1965 (Reprint by Southern Publishing Co., Delray Beach, FL)

Burland, Cottie *North American Indian Mythology*, Paul Hamlyn Limited, Drury House, London, 1965

Burt, Jesse and Ferguson, Robert B. *Indians of the Southwest: Then and Now* Abington Press, Nashville & NY, 1973

Coe, Charles H. *Red Patriots: The Story of the Seminoles* University Press of Florida, Gainesville, FL, 1974

Coe, Michael D. *Breaking the Maya Code* Thames & Hudson, 1992

Cotterill, R. S. *The Southern Indians—The Story of Civilized Tribes Before Removal* University of Oklahoma Press, Norman, OK, 1954

Covington, James W., Editor *Pirates, Indians and Spaniards* Translated by A. F. Falcones Great Outdoors Publishing Co., St. Petersburg, FL, 1963

Covington, James W. *The Billy Bowlegs War: 1855-1858 The Final Stand of the Seminoles Against the Whites.* Mickler House 1982

Covington, James W. *The Seminoles of Florida* University Press of Florida, Gainesville, FL, 1993

Douglas, Marjory Stoneman *The Everglades, River of Grass* N.Y. Rinehart, 1947

Emerson, William C. *The Seminoles: Dwellers of the Everglades* Exposition Press, Inc. N.Y., N.Y., 1954

Ervin, William R. *The Seminole War: Prelude to Victory 1823-1838* W. & S. Ervin, Holly Hill, FL, 1983

Fairbanks, Charles H. *The Florida Seminole People* Indian Tribal Series, Phoenix, AZ, 1973

Farb, Peter *Man's Rise to Civilization: The Cultural Ascent of the Indians of North America* E. P. Dutton, NY, 1968

Fash, William *Scribes, Warriors and Kings* Thames and Hudson, 1991

Francke, Arthur, E. Jr. *Fort Mellon 1837-42: a Microcosm of the Second Seminole War* Banyan Books, Inc. Miami, FL, 1977

Gaddis, Vincent H. *American Indian Myths and Mysteries* Chilton Book Company, Radnor, PA, IY77

Garbarino, Merwyn S. *Big Cypress: A Changing Seminole Comunity* New York Holt Rinehart & Winston, IY72

Garbarino, Merwyn S. *Indians of North Anerica, The Seminole* Chelsea House Publishers, N.Y., 1989

Glenn, James Lafayette *My Work Among the Florida Seminoles* edited by Harry A. Kersey, University Presses of Florida, Orlando, FL, 1982

Hartley, William B. *Osceola, the Unconquered Indian* Hawthorn Books, NY, 1973

Kearney, Bob *Mostly Sunny Days* A *Miami Herald* Salute to South Florida's Heritage Suniland Press, Miami, FL, 1986

Kersey, Harry A. Jr. *The Florida Seminoles and the New Deal 1933-1942* Florida Atlantic University Press, Boca Raton, FL, 1989

Kersey, Harry A. Jr. *Pelts, Plumes and Hides: White Traders Among the Seminole Indians 1870-1930* University Presses of Florida, 1975

Laumer, Frank *Massacre!* University of Florida Press, Gainesville, FL, 1968

Lawson, Edith Ridenour *Florida Indians: Noble Redmen of the South* Valkyrie Press, Inc., St. Petersburg, FL, 1977

Littlefield, Daniel F., Jr. *Africans and Seminoles: From Removal to Emancipation* Greenwood Press, Westport, CT, l977

Mahon, John K. *History of the Second Seminole War* University of Florida Press, Jacksonville, FL, 1967

Mancini, Richard E. *Indians of the Southeast* Facts on File, NY, 1992

239

McGoun, William E. *Prehistoric Peoples of South Florida* The University of Alabama Press, Tuscaloosa, Alabama and London, 1993

McIver, Stuart B. *Yesterday's Palm Beach* E. A. Seemann Publishing , Inc. Miaml, FL, 1976

McIver, Stuart *True Tales of the Everglades* Florida Flair Books, Miami, FL, 1989

McReynolds, Edwin C. *The Seminoles* Norman Press, University of Oklahoma, 1957

Milanich, Jerald and Proctor, Samuel *Tacachale* University of Florida Press, Gainesville, FL, 1978

Moore-Willson, Minnie *Osceola* The Davies publishing Co., Inc., Palm Beach, FL, 1931

Moore-Willson, Minnie *The Seminoles of Florida* Kingsport Press, Kingsport, TN, 1928

Neill, Wilfred T. *The Story of Florida's Seminole Indians* Great Outdoors Publishing Co., St. Petersburg, FL, 1956

Nicholas, James C. *Recommendations concerning employment, income, and educational opportunities for the Seminole and Miccosukee Tribes in Florida* Hollywood, FL, U.S. Dept. of the Interior, Bureau of Indian Affairs, 1974

Patrick, Rembert W. *Florida Under Five Flags* University of Florida Press, Gainesville, FL, 1955

Peithmann, Irvin M. *The Unconquered Seminole Indians* Great Outdoors Publishing Co., St. Petersburg, FL, 1947

Peters, Virginia Bergman *The Florida Wars* Archon Books, Hamden, CT, 1979

Proctor, Samuel, General Editor *A Narrative of the Early Days and Remembrances of Osceola Nikkanochee* The Bicentennial Floridiana Facsimile Series, A University of Florida Book 1977

Schele, Linda and Mary Miller *Blood of Kings: Dynasty and Ritual in Ancient Art* Fort Worth, 1986

Scherer, Joanna Cohan *Indians* Crown publishers, 1973

Sheehan, Neil *A Bright Shining Lie* John Paul Vann and America in Vietnam Random House, NY, 1988

Starkey, Marion L. *The Cherokee Nation* Alfred A. Knopf, NY, 1946

Stephens, John *Incidents of Travel in Central America, Chiapas and Yucatan* Harper Brothers, New York, 1841

Thompson, J. Eric *The Rise and Fall of Maya Civilization* University of Oklahoma Press, Norman, OK, 1954

Walton, George *Fearless and Free: The Seminole War 1835-1842* Bobbs Merrill, N.Y., 1977

Weaver, Muriel *The Aztecs, Maya and Their Predecessors* Second Edition, New York, 1981

Weisman, Brent *Like Beads on a String: A Cultural History of the Seminole Indians in Northern Peninsular Florida* University of Alabama Press, Tuscaloosa, AL 1989

Wickman, Patricia Riles *Osceola's Legacy* University of Alabama Press, Tuscaloosa, AL, 1991

Willoughby, Hugh Laussat *Across the Everglades: A Canoe Journey of Exploration* J. B. Lippincott Company, N.Y., 1898

Wilson, Charles J. *The Indian Presence* Archeology of Santibel, Captiva and Adjacent Islands in Pine Island Sound, Captiva Conservation Foundation, Sanibel Island, FL, 1982

Wissler, Clark *Indians of the United States; Four Centuries of Their History and Culture* Doubleday, Doran and Company, Inc., NY, 1940

Wright, J. Leitch *Creeks and Seminoles - The Destruction and Regeneration of the Muscogulge People* University of Nebraska Press, Lincoln, NB, 1986

Yenne, Bill *The Encyclopedia of North American Indian Tribes; A Comprehensive Study of Tribes from the Abitibi to the Zuni* Crescent Books, N.Y., 1986

INDEX

A

B

C

D-E-F

g

ℑ

U-Z

***

Typographic note:
The body of text in this book was set
in 11.5 point ITC New Baskerville